16.95

VGM Professional Careers Series

CAREERS
IN JOURNALISM

JAN GOLDBERG

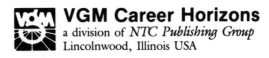

VGM Career Horizons
a division of *NTC Publishing Group*
Lincolnwood, Illinois USA

Cover photo courtesy of *The Blade*, Toledo, Ohio.

Library of Congress Cataloging-in-Publication Data

Goldberg, Jan
    Careers in journalism/Jan Goldberg.
      p. cm. — (VGM professional career series)
    Includes bibliographical references.
    ISBN 0-8442-4196-2 (hard). — ISBN 0-8442-4197-0 (pbk.)
    1. Journalsim—Vocational guidance. I. Title. II. Series.
PN4797.G58 1995
070.4'023—dc20   94-20145
                                           CIP

Published by VGM Career Horizons, a division of NTC Publishing Group
4255 West Touhy Avenue
Lincolnwood (Chicago), Illinois 60646-1975, U.S.A.

4 5 6 7 8 9 0 VP 9 8 7 6 5 4 3 2 1

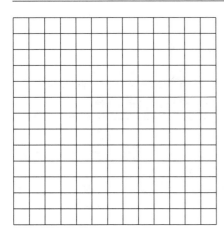

CONTENTS

**PART ONE   INTRODUCTION TO THE WORLD OF
                          JOURNALISM**

      Is journalism for you? What does journalism encompass?
      Variety is the spice of life.

      In the beginning. The American way. A new nation. The penny
      press. Press associations. Newspapers go to war. The new
      journalism. The Canadian press. A new era. The Jazz Age.
      Journalism today.

PART TWO   CAREER CHOICES IN JOURNALISM

      Reporters and correspondents. Investigative journalists.
      Columnists. Editorial writers. Photojournalists and news
      camerapersons. Editorial cartoonists. Editors. Copy editors.
      Proofreaders. Major U.S. newspapers. Major Canadian
      newspapers.

PART FOUR   BEGINNING YOUR CAREER

Goal setting. Looking for opportunities. Preparing for a job
search. Interviewing. Tests. Following up. Building a career.

ABOUT THE AUTHOR

Jan Goldberg's love affair with the printed page began well before her second birthday. Regular visits to the book bindery where her grandfather worked produced a magic of sights and smells that she carries with her to this day.

Childhood was filled with composing poems and stories, reading books or "playing library." Elementary and high school included a vast assortment of contributions to school newspapers. While a full-time college student, Goldberg wrote extensively as part of her job responsibilities in the College of Business Administration at Roosevelt University in Chicago. After receiving a degree in elementary education, she was able to extend her love of reading and writing to her students.

Beginning her career as a poet, Goldberg's work appeared in *Bell's Letters, Complete Woman,* and a number of poetry anthologies. She won several awards, including first place in a *Bell's Letters* contest. Following that, her varied career branched into book reviews for several periodicals, including *The Bloomsbury Review.*

Goldberg serves as a media consultant for a local park district, composing media releases as well as handling special projects and newsletters. She has also completed numerous projects in marketing and public relations for the Jewish Community Centers of Chicago and serves as a writer for Lekas and Levine Public Relations.

In the area of business writing, Goldberg has been a regular contributor to The Dartnell Corporation for the past five years. She authors pamphlets, bimonthly articles, and quizzes for six sales instructional and motivational publications and also writes for a management-level newsletter.

Goldberg has written extensively in the occupations area for General Learning Corporation's *Career World Magazine*, and the many career publications produced by CRS Recruitment Publications. She has also worked on a number of projects for educational publishers, such as Scott Foresman and Britannica Learning Centers, including textbooks for reading and science and the creation of a literature-based reading/writing program.

As a feature writer, Goldberg's work has appeared in *Today's Chicago Woman, Opportunity Magazine, Chicago Parent,* the Pioneer Press newspapers, *Complete Woman,* and *North Shore Magazine.* Several monthly North Shore cable television programs have been based on her articles. In all, she has authored more than 200 published pieces as a full-time freelance writer.

ACKNOWLEDGMENTS

The author gratefully acknowledges
- The fifteen professionals who graciously agreed to be profiled herein
- The following individuals and organizations for their assistance and information:

    Lee Becker, School of Journalism, The Ohio State University

    R. Ehrgott, Associate Editor, QUILL

    Society of Professional Journalists

    American Society of Magazine Editors

    Society for Technical Communication

    Newspaper Association of America Foundation

    National Newspaper Foundation

    American Society of Newspaper Editors Foundation

    Magazine Publishers of America

    The Dow Jones Newspaper Fund, Inc.

    Accrediting Council on Education in Journalism and Mass Communications

    National Association of Broadcasters

    The Newspaper Guild

    University of Chicago Publishing Program

    Radcliffe Publishing Course

    Stanford Publishing Course

- My dear husband, Larry, and daughters, Sherri and Debbie, for their unending patience, love, and encouragement
- Family and close friends for their love and support: Mom, Adrienne, Marty, Bruce, Paul, Michele, Alison, Steven, Marci, Paul, Steven, Brian, Jesse, Bertha, and Ralph
- A special thanks to a special friend, Diana Catlin, for her insights and input
- Sincere gratitude to Anne Knudsen, executive editor at VGM, for providing this challenging opportunity, and Sarah Kennedy, editor at VGM, for making the project such a rewarding and enjoyable experience.

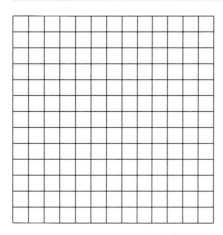

DEDICATION

TO: My husband, Larry,
for providing me with everything I need.

TO: My daughters, Sherri and Debbie,
for continually rooting me on.

TO: The memory of my mother, Sylvia Lefkovitz,
who was *always* there for me.

TO: My memory of my father, Sam Lefkovitz,
who always gave me a warm glow
and a reason to smile.

Part One
Introduction to
The World of Journalism

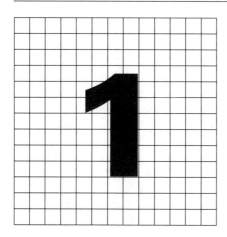

WHY CHOOSE JOURNALISM?

Writing, like life itself, is a voyage of discovery.
—Henry Miller

Why is grass green? How do birds fly? Who discovered the South Pole? What is furniture made of? Why does thunder make noise? How do fish live under water? Where do squirrels live? When was the Emancipation Proclamation written? Who is smarter—men or women? And on and on and on. If this endless stream of questions sounds incredibly reminiscent of you during childhood and beyond, you are a likely candidate for a career in journalism.*

Many qualities are common to journalists but at the core is an insatiable curiosity *about virtually anything and everything*. All topics and areas are fodder for investigation: what is seen (or unseen); all that you can put your finger on and much that you cannot; the multitudes of systems that exist within us and all that is outside, including relationships between people, cities, nations, planets, and galaxies. The journalistic spirit recognizes and eagerly anticipates exploring the wealth and depth of information that is already available in addition to all that remains to be discovered.

IS JOURNALISM FOR YOU?

People enter journalism for a variety of reasons. Some feel it represents a glamorous, easy, well-paid career. Others feel they are innately talented and enjoy research and reporting. In reality, journalism in all its forms is hard work, is rarely glamorous, and certainly doesn't always offer a high salary or standard of living. It is folly to consider entering this field because someone

---

*There are varying definitions of the word *journalism*. In its strictest sense, the word refers only to the newspaper and, perhaps, magazine industries. For the purposes of this book, however, journalism is interpreted in its broadest sense to include all the careers that an individual with a love for words and the expression of ideas may explore.

in your family was a journalist or is pushing you to become one. Without sufficient desire and drive, you won't succeed in this profession.

All journalists are communicators who work hard to transmit their ideas and information. In endeavoring to present a point of view, make readers more aware or better educated, and/or entertain them, the challenge is to consistently provide material that is concise, easily understood and of a high caliber. No matter what their area, journalists spend their entire professional lives working to perfect their craft.

With the vastness and sophistication of mass communications today, a writer's audience may range in the hundreds, thousands, or even millions. This places journalists in a potentially powerful position. By bringing their words to others, they are able to promote and effect change in individuals, groups, and society as a whole. In fact, they can even make the world a better place.

If you remain unsure of your occupational destination but feel that somehow words are the vehicle to transport you there, a career in journalism is a wise and soul-fulfilling choice.

WHAT DOES JOURNALISM ENCOMPASS?

In the fictional town of Journalismville, members of the community work at their respective careers:

Larry appears every night as the six o'clock news anchor. Diana writes a mystery novel. Bruce creates programs for computers. Debbie writes sales articles for a business publisher. Michele is a children's book editor. Paul writes speeches for a U.S. Senator. Adrienne teaches creative writing at the local junior college. Mindi writes media releases for a public relations firm. Marci proofreads manuscripts for a scientific magazine. Marty writes copy for his advertising clients. Steven is a photojournalist for the local newspaper. Alison creates employee manuals and newsletters for large corporations. Cary authors a column for the daily newspaper. Sylvia is a copywriter. Sherri is writing a biography on Michael Jordan.

What do these people have in common? *All of them have chosen careers in journalism.*

VARIETY IS THE SPICE OF LIFE

Careers in journalism are many and varied but all are based on bringing a message to others. Much of this is accomplished through mass communications media—radio, television, newspapers, books, and magazines. Whether oral or written, journalists choose words and place them in carefully designed combinations to give the reader insights, information, or entertainment (or perhaps all three). Sometimes visual pieces are presented and arranged to accomplish the same goals.

Newspaper publishing

Many journalists choose careers in newspaper publishing. Depending on the size of the newspaper, they may serve as editors (from editors-in-chief to assistant editors), specialty editors (religious, financial, or fashion, for example), columnists, syndicated columnists, investigative journalists, feature writers, editorial writers, reporters, correspondents, photojournalists, editorial cartoonists, copy editors, or proofreaders. Of course, smaller newspapers have fewer employees, calling for individuals to perform a number of functions and assume several roles.

A newspaper journalist may also choose to work for a wire service, such as Associated Press (AP) or United Press International (UPI), in the capacity of reporter or "stringer."

Magazine publishing

Magazine publishing is another vast communications medium that employs large numbers of journalists. Similar to newspapers, established magazines may maintain a hierarchy of editors, including managing editors, executive editors, associate editors, assistant editors, department editors (travel or lifestyle, for example), editorial assistants, feature writers, article authors, columnists, copy editors, and proofreaders. Freelance writers may provide additional feature articles, fiction, short stories, and poems.

Book publishing

For book publishers, journalists may serve as editors of either hardbound or paperback books (again at varying levels of title and responsibility), editorial assistants, copy editors, and proofreaders.

Books themselves are most often written by freelance writers who do not actually work for the publishing company but are under contract. This includes nonfiction and fiction authors who may choose to write for a juvenile or adult audience in a variety of genres, including science fiction, horror, romance, or mystery.

A large segment of the book industry is involved in elementary, secondary, or college textbook publishing, and in this area, journalists usually work as part of a large team of individuals including writers, editors, copywriters, and proofreaders who take a book from idea to finished manuscript.

Electronic media

Television and radio provide other potential sources of employment for journalists who enjoy appearing in front of a camera or providing behind-the-scenes back-up. Broadcast journalists (reporters); anchors; editors at various levels; sportscasters; newscasters or announcers; and television, cable, video, and radio scriptwriters all contribute to the smooth operation of this medium.

Technical writing

In the technical areas, journalists most often create instructional sheets, directions, and manuals that enable nonprofessionals to understand how to operate sophisticated technical equipment. Thus, journalists with a strong understanding of the world of computers will no doubt have ample opportunities to create software or write about issues relating to computers and software. Other options include writing about scientific, mathematical, agricultural, medical, or engineering issues for newspapers or specialty or general consumer magazines; writing books; or authoring speeches or news releases of a scientific nature.

Educational possibilities

For those who enjoy working with children, young adults, or adults, and who delight in passing their wisdom and methods on to others, careers in teaching are attractive. Journalism, communication, English, and creative writing classes, seminars, workshops, and correspondence programs are offered at high school, junior college, undergraduate, and advanced degree levels. This opens up the possibility of a career in journalism through teaching at any of these levels.

Business writing

The area of business writing presents a lucrative and prolific career for many journalists. Companies and corporations, clubs, nonprofit organizations, and other groups employ journalists to write articles, sales letters, brochures, newsletters, employee manuals, business reports, and direct-mail projects. Many journalists also enter related fields, such as public relations or advertising.

Other Options

Rounding out the list of diverse journalistic possibilities are careers in speech writing, poetry, songwriting, ghostwriting, freelance writing, book reviewing, comedy writing, playwriting, and screenwriting. Opportunities also exist for literary agents. Here's another thought: If solving riddles is your passion, consider a career as a crossword puzzle editor!

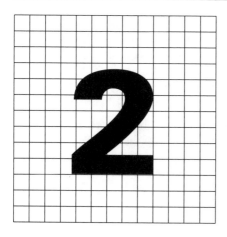

JOURNALISM FROM AN HISTORICAL PERSPECTIVE

Literature is the art of writing something that will be read twice; journalism what will be grasped at once.

—Cyril Connolly

Our forefathers traveled to the New World and instituted changes that left us the legacy of a free press and the right to free speech. Leaving nothing to chance, they drafted the U.S. Constitution's first amendment to read, "Congress shall make no law respecting an establishment of religion, or prohibiting the free exercise thereof; or abridging the freedom of speech, or of the press; or the right of the people peaceably to assemble, and to petition the Government for a redress of grievances." Thus, the principles of free press and free speech became part of the American heritage through the ratification of the Bill of Rights in 1791.

Similarly, in 1982, a Canadian Constitution guaranteed to Canadians "the liberties of an open society with a free and vigorous press." This document confirmed in writing what had long been a tradition in Canada.

But freedom of the press did not always exist and still is absent in many areas of the world today. The delegates who drafted the Constitution remembered how the injustices of the British Crown had been revealed to the public through the press and how the press had stirred revolutionary feelings in the colonists. They realized that the press was at least partially responsible for arousing enough intensity and emotion to prompt the colonists to take action.

One statesman who understood the importance of a free press was Thomas Jefferson. In 1787, he wrote to his friend, Carrington:

I am persuaded that the good sense of the people will always be found to be the best army. They may be led astray for a moment, but will soon correct themselves. The people are the only censors of their governors; and even their errors will tend to keep these to the true principles of their institution. To punish these errors too severely would be to suppress the only safeguard of the public liberty. The way to prevent these irregular interpositions of the people, is to give them full information of their affairs through the channel of the public papers, and to contrive that those papers should penetrate the whole mass of the people. The basis of our government being the opinion of the people, the very first object should be to keep that right; and were it left to me to decide whether we should have a government without newspapers, or newspapers without a government, I should not hesitate a moment to prefer the latter.

Today, North American newspapers, magazines, books, radio, television, films, and other communications media flourish with the freedom to provide whatever news and information is deemed appropriate by writers and editors. Thus, the work of a journalist is firmly rooted in history.

IN THE BEGINNING

Without question, the invention of the printing press brought about profound and far-reaching changes in the course of history. Many regard it as one of the most significant inventions of all time. Certainly its birth provided an opportunity to offer education and literacy to the masses. Without it, there could have been no Industrial Revolution, and we would not be experiencing the electronic revolution and Information Age of today.

Although there is no historical certainty, most authorities credit a German, Johannes Gutenberg, with inventing the printing press. His Gutenberg Bible, which appeared about 1454, is traditionally recognized as the very first book printed using movable type. From Germany, printing spread to other countries, namely France, Italy, Spain, and Switzerland. It was introduced to England by William Caxton, a native of Kent. As England's first printer, he is remembered for publishing some of the major literature of the time. During a 15-year period, he produced approximately 100 volumes. In contrast to many printers in other countries who used only Latin, Caxton published all of his material in his native language, English.

THE AMERICAN WAY

America saw its first printing press about 200 years later in 1638. Reverend Jesse Glover was responsible for its transfer from England and its establishment in the Massachusetts Bay Colony at Cambridge. His associate, Stephen Daye, and his son, Matthew, set up the printing press at Harvard College after Glover died during the journey from England. The Dayes' first printed work was called *Freeman's Oath*. In 1640, they produced their first book, the *Bay Psalm Book*.

In the New World, most presses published both books and newspapers. The first American newspaper was produced by Benjamin Harris in 1690 in Boston. Called *Publick Occurrences Both Forreign and Domestick*, the paper survived only one day before it was closed by the British government. Harris, who had fled England because the stories he printed there created such a stir, was told he must stop printing in America because he had no license. Though this was true, it is likely that his real transgression was printing an article that was offensive to the king of France, the colonies' longtime ally.

After Harris' aborted newspaper attempt, it was 14 years before a second newspaper was published in the colonies. Postmaster John Campbell produced the *Boston News-Letter* in 1704 and continued without competition for 15 years. Since he was loyal to the Crown, he was allowed to publish his newspaper undisturbed.

Colonial newspapers were disorganized and limited in circulation. This is not surprising since the first newspaper publishers were really printers rather than editors. They were not educated men and certainly not journalists as we interpret the word now. Many understood what was important to people, but only a handful had the instincts of a reporter. Also, their access to obtaining news was severely limited by poor transportation and communication devices. Most didn't even make an attempt to seek out items of news interest and were satisfied to write about things they happened upon. None employed local reporters, even during the revolutionary war when only papers nearest the scene of an event would cover a story. After that, other publications copied the piece or included reprinted official announcements, military or governmental correspondence, or information from travelers.

An individual who did show some writing ability was an early editor and printer named James Franklin. He was the publisher of the third colonial newspaper, the *New England Courant*, which debuted in 1721. Clearly better than his competition, Franklin provided a readable and interesting product. His newspaper included human interest articles, personality sketches, literate feature stories, and articles signed "Silence Dogood" (a pen name used by Franklin's brother Benjamin). By publishing articles critical of the British Crown, Franklin's outspoken nature made him the first to challenge the rigid licensing system that controlled the colonial press. It was Franklin who established the press as an instrument that could clearly both reflect and influence popular opinion. As a result of his criticism, he was imprisoned. While there, his brother Benjamin assumed the position of editor of the *New England Courant*. Benjamin was a talented writer whose work was informative and entertaining. Unfortunately, Benjamin's success caused dissension among the brothers, prompting Benjamin to move to New York.

In 1729, Benjamin Franklin established a new paper in Philadelphia, the *Pennsylvania Gazette*. Almost immediately, it became a success. This publication and *The American Weekly Mercury* published by Andrew Bradford were the first newspapers to appear outside New England.

In 1733, Bradford's former assistant, John Peter Zenger, founded the *New York Weekly Journal*. Since the paper was heavily procolonist and anti-Crown, it was very popular in America but quite a thorn in the side of the British colonial leaders, particularly Governor William Cosby. Several factors, including the fact that Zenger criticized Governor Cosby for permitting French naval units to settle in New York Harbor, prompted Cosby to initiate proceedings against Zenger. In November of 1734, he was arrested and charged with criminal libel. While he spent months in jail, his wife continued to print the paper.

Zenger was ably defended by octogenarian Andrew Hamilton, a famous Philadelphia lawyer who offered his services. Basing his defense on the premise of a free press, Hamilton argued that Zenger could not be guilty unless what he stated in print was actually libelous. That would mean that the words themselves must include malicious or seditious (inciting rebellion against a government) falsehoods. Prior to this trial, guilt was based on the printing of any seditious statement, whether it was true or false. The jury found Zenger not guilty, and the chief justice did not intervene by setting aside the verdict even though he had the power to do so. It was a great moral victory for Hamilton and established a principle that is still in effect today. Libel only exists when falsehoods are perpetrated; the truth can never be libelous.

In Canada, as a colony of the centralized Bourbon French monarchy, New France was not permitted a printing press until 1760. In the wake of the British expedition to found Halifax, printing came to Nova Scotia in 1751 and to Quebec in 1764, after the British conquest. The beginnings of journalism were largely ineffective due to the widespread illiteracy and limited circulations of publications. Just as in the thirteen colonies, most journalists were publishers, editors, and printers all in one. Also, Canadian journalists could be arrested and publishers convicted of criminal or seditious libel for criticizing public officials.

Back in the colonies, the Stamp Act of 1765 was considered a real blow to the American free press since it put a substantial tax on paper used in producing newspapers and legal documents. Both journalists and lawyers were very offended by it, and as a result newspapers began to argue the philosophy of the revolution.

One of the militant newspapers of the time was the *Boston Gazette*. Frequently published in this paper was Samuel Adams, a journalist who wrote tirelessly and prolifically with increasing hatred for the British. His stories included accounts of British soldiers beating children and raping young women (accusations denied by the British). Known as a propagandist for the revolution, many historians believe he is responsible for the attack of British soldiers which ultimately led to the Boston Massacre in 1770. Adams was called the "assassin of reputations" and "master of the puppets" by his adversaries. It is said that when important news was not present, he exaggerated minor incidents to make them look like major events.

Thomas Paine, the well-known political philosopher, came to the colonies in time to offer two printed contributions to the patriot cause. *Common Sense*, his well-known argument for independence aimed at the common man, sold 12,000 copies in the spring of 1776. In December of that year, Paine crafted the first of his Crisis papers when Washington's army was dejectedly positioned on the Delaware.

By 1775, the press had become increasingly partisan and screamed for a beginning to the war.

A NEW NATION

Journalistically speaking, the period after the Revolution was undistinguished although two types of newspapers were developing. One was printed in the towns along the seacoast primarily for shippers and traders. Included in these publications were articles concerning politics and commerce. They also contained advertising columns that reflected the business interests of their limited readership (about 2,000). The other type was politically partisan and was marked by the press's (often undeserved) targeting of high officials, such as John Adams, Thomas Jefferson, Alexander Hamilton, and George Washington. In fact, besides Richard Nixon, George Washington's relationship with the press is considered one of the worst of any president.

From 1787 to 1788, Alexander Hamilton, the outstanding leader of the pro-Constitution party, coauthored the *Federalist Papers* for the newspapers of New York state. Subsequently, they were reprinted all over the country. A series of 85 articles, this work is considered one of the best political treatises ever written. Hamilton is also known for establishing the *New York Post* in 1801. It is the oldest continuously published daily newspaper in the United States.

In the early 1800s, individual papers changed their policies and began to go out and seek information to include in their publications. As early as 1808, correspondents were sent to Washington to report the news of the day. Representatives from the seaport newspapers met incoming ships to get a head start on foreign happenings. The leading New York mercantile papers, the *Journal of Commerce*, and the *Courier and Enquirer* set up pony express systems to "scoop" one another on congressional and presidential news.

By 1825, there were several hundred newspapers in America. In most cases, they were handled by subscriptions amounting to anywhere from six to ten dollars. Since these fees had to be paid in advance, only wealthy people were able to afford them.

THE PENNY PRESS

In 1833, Benjamin Day created a sensation when he launched the first successful penny newspaper, the *New York Sun*. This publication was bright and readable and represented a revolutionary new idea in the newspaper industry: a publication designed for the masses, something the "common man" could afford and enjoy. No longer did the newspaper have to rely on business interests or political parties. The *Sun* emphasized local news and was a success almost immediately. It tended to look for the sensational, emphasizing accounts of crime and sex that were obtained from the police reporter Day hired to cover crime news.

Day also became an innovator in the marketing area when he placed newsboys on the streets to sell his papers. (They were sold to the boys for 67 cents per hundred.) Since competitors were selling their papers for six cents, Day had a decided advantage. The *New York Sun* prospered and tripled its circulation by 1835.

This is the same year that Canada experienced the libel case of Joseph Howe. In his paper, *The Novascotian* (acquired in 1827), Howe criticized both public policies and the policy makers. In a case reminiscent of Zenger's, he was indicted for criminal libel and sent to jail. Defending himself at his trial, he presented evidence to substantiate his criticism and spoke with great passion of the virtues of a free press. Although he was clearly guilty (as was Zenger), he too was acquitted.

The 1830s and 1840s saw the emergence of the penny press as a respectable newspaper daily in the United States. Some strong personalities came on the scene to make their mark on the history of journalism.

One such man was James Gordon Bennett who observed Day's success and founded the *New York Herald* in 1835. Bennett was clearly a reporter and editor, not a printer as many had been before him. The *Herald* included news of Wall Street, foreign countries, religion, the theater, and society, and always displayed a sincere attempt to present an objective viewpoint. Although Bennett, too, sought the sensational, he understood the importance of being the first to print a story and thus employed correspondents, made use of the telegraph, and even hired locomotives to quickly bring presidential messages from Washington to scoop his opponents. His efforts were rewarded. By 1860, the *Herald* was the world's largest newspaper with a readership of over 77,000.

Others saw the potential of these newspapers, and a number of competitors appeared. One of the most able was Horace Greeley who established his *New York Tribune* in 1841. Shunning the sensational, Greeley covered the news fairly and focused on the editorial page. As a man of integrity, he espoused his views against slavery and in favor of other humanitarian issues, and he is known as the first oustanding liberal editor and one of the most influential in the history of American journalism. In fact, he has been called "the father of American journalism."

Meanwhile, in Canada, journalists were commonly allying themselves with political parties. In 1844, the Reform Party convinced George Brown to establish the *Toronto Globe*. Brown's influence enhanced the *Globe's* advertising revenue and increased the paper's circulation. As his power increased, he became the leader of the reconstituted Grit Reform Party after 1854. This gave him a great amount of journalistic freedom to say what he wished. Two other successful newspaper tycoons, Etienne Parent of *Le Canadien* and Edward Whelan of the *Charlottetown Examiner*, also enjoyed great editorial freedom due to their roles as publisher-politicians.

Back in the United States, another important newspaper that sprang up at this time was the *New York Times*, established in 1851 by Henry Jarvis Raymond and George Jones. Distinctively, it presented a moderate point of view and avoided scandal. After Raymond's death, the circulation declined until 1896, when it was taken over by Adolph Ochs. Raising the caliber of the paper to a high level, Ochs brought success back to the *Times*. On rescuing the paper from bankruptcy, Ochs told his readers, "It will be my aim...to give the news impartially, without fear or favor..." Today the *Times* is considered the best newspaper in the United States, perhaps in the world.

PRESS ASSOCIATIONS

It became apparent that no one newspaper could individually seek out, collect, and report all of the news, so in 1848 six New York newspapers joined together under the name of Associated Press of New York. With the aim of sharing the expenses of procuring both national and international news, this association became the forerunner of today's press associations, such as the Associated Press (AP) and United Press International (UPI). These services function with the same purpose today.

NEWSPAPERS GO TO WAR

The popularity of newspapers was given a boost by the Civil War because readers were interested in finding out the daily details of happenings on the battlefields. It also intensified the breach between the North and the South. Gone was the sense of oneness that had existed since the Revolution. Again the presses often became partisan, espousing only their particular point of view, even to the point of promoting bigotry and hate. The results of the war were to increase newspaper circulation, demonstrate the success of the press associations, and increase the importance of war correspondents.

THE NEW JOURNALISM

In the world of newspapers, 1865 to 1900 is known as a period of "The New Journalism." Great changes were taking place in the United States, including doubling the population, quadrupling the national wealth, and increasing the production of manufacturing sevenfold. With the invention of the telephone, typewriter, and electric light bulb in the 1880s, communication systems were vastly improved.

THE CANADIAN PRESS

By the 1880s, a new type of newspaper had appeared in Canada. Called the "people's journals," the publications quickly developed a large circulation in the northern industrial cities. Abandoning political ties and emphasizing opinion rather than news, the papers focused on the sensationalism that was common in the colonies. The excellence of papers such as the *Toronto Mail* and the *Montreal Gazette* vied for readership by presenting articles detailing political and business activities.

By the turn of the century, professional editors such as John W. DaFoe of the *Manitoba Free Press* were in evidence, and women were given an opportunity to enter the world of journalism; Edouardina Lesage ("Collette") at *La Presse* and Kit Coleman at the *Mail and Empire* initiated careers in the new "women's sections."

A NEW ERA

In 1878, Joseph Pulitzer, an outstanding man and Hungarian immigrant, came to America and established the *St. Louis Post-Dispatch*. Over the next five years, he catapulted it to success by emphasizing an aggressive approach both on the editorial and news pages. He promoted good writing and insisted on printing only proven facts.

Leaving St. Louis in 1883, Pulitzer moved to New York and purchased the *New York World*, a poorly performing newspaper. Four years later, the *World's* circulation had climbed to 250,000, and it had surpassed the *Herald* in advertising. This was a result of Pulitzer's devotion to journalistic integrity. The *World* carried solid news and human interest features, illustrations, and a measure of sensationalism. Pulitzer was a friend to workers and small businessmen and championed their cause no matter whose authority it challenged. He instituted the political cartoon, the first of which, drawn by Richard Outcault, was called "The Yellow Kid." When color printing came into being in the early 1890s, the *World* added comic strips. The first to produce a Sunday paper, Pulitzer also created today's familiar Sunday supplements.

Coming on the scene to challenge Pulitzer during the mid-1890s was William Randolph Hearst, who bought the *New York Morning Journal* in 1895. Hearst so admired Pulitzer that he hired Putlizer's entire Sunday paper staff. Pulitzer got them back by making them a better offer but Hearst countered with more money and the staff left again; this time staying at the *Journal* for good. Pulitzer hired a new staff knowing that he faced a fierce competitor.

Both Pulitzer and Hearst made contributions to the growth of American journalism. They both fought for the causes of the common man and for issues that would help society. With the popularity of their publications, they had a hand in influencing public opinion, particularly in the matter of the Spanish American War. Both printed highly inflammatory articles favoring war with Spain. Critics coined this type of writing *yellow journalism*, which became a phrase used to symbolize emotional, sensational news.

Once the war was over, Pulitzer turned away from the competition and concentrated on the quality of his newspaper. His most lasting gifts are considered to be the prizes he established in his name at Columbia University's School of Journalism in 1911. Today, the Pulitzer Prize remains the most prestigious award in the world of journalism. Many outstanding journalists in the United States and Canada have received this award. Notably, John M. Imrie of the *Edmonton Journal* was honored with a Pulitzer in 1937 for his leadership in the fight against the Alberta Press Act, which sought to challenge the freedom of the press.

THE JAZZ AGE

The 1920s were known as the "Jazz Age," a reference to the newspapers of this era that exploited sensationalism to the point of being irresponsible. Usually these publications focused heavily on photographs and appeared in a tabloid format. This brand of journalism was led by the *New York Illustrated Daily News*, established in 1919 by Joseph Medill Patterson, cousin of Robert R. McCormick and partner with him in publishing the *Chicago Tribune*. By 1924, the *Daily News* enjoyed the largest newspaper circulation in the country, a position it held until it was surpassed by the *Wall Street Journal* in 1980.

JOURNALISM TODAY

In order to stay afloat in recent times, there has been a trend for a number of newspapers to merge together. The Gannett chain, for instance, consists of more than 100 papers and is best known for *USA Today*.

Although investigative reporting is not a new phenomenon, it has been raised to the status of a fine art. Heading the list of eminent achievements in this area is the uncovering, discovering, and reporting of the Watergate scandal by *Washington Post* reporters, Bob Woodward and Carl Bernstein. In 1973, the *Washington Post* was awarded a Pulitzer Prize for outstanding work for the public good. Also noteworthy is the *New York Times*'s account of "The Pentagon Papers." Both exposés showed that the power of the press is as strong today as it ever was.

With the addition of radio in 1916, sound movies in 1926, and television in 1939, three more formidable media opponents entered the mass communications market. Though many print casualties resulted from these and other social and economic factors, newspapers magazines, and books remain an important part of life in North America.

Part Two
Career Choices in Journalism

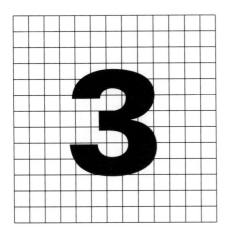

NEWSPAPER PUBLISHING

For Godsake, keep your eyes open. Notice what's going on around you.

—William Burroughs

Clark Kent, mild-mannered reporter for the *Daily Planet* in Metropolis, judiciously covered news events as they unfolded, donning his Superman garb whenever he was called on to fight for "truth, justice, and the American way." His boss, Editor-in-Chief Perry White, provided leads, words of wisdom, and a measure of curmudgeonly advice. Working together, Kent, trusted co-reporter Lois Lane, and friend and photographer Jimmy Olsen provided the news for the citizens of Metropolis.

This was all pure fantasy, of course. In the real world, Superman is not at hand to prevent disaster, catch transgressors, and right the wrongs of the world. But, aside from typewriters being replaced by computers, the process of reporting the news as Clark Kent and Lois Lane did remains strikingly similar. And although it takes many professionals in various capacities to produce a newspaper, the foundation on which everything else rests is the reporter.

REPORTERS AND CORRESPONDENTS

Like Clark Kent, the thousands of reporters (sometimes referred to as news writers) who work for newspapers in the United States and Canada are responsible for the same activities: gathering facts and reporting them to the public. They accomplish this through interviews, news briefings, printed reports, letters, question-and-answer sessions, news conferences, individual research and intelligent and persistent use of the telephone. Reporters often go to the scene of an incident to find out as much as possible about the details of the event. There they take extensive notes and interview involved individuals, usually taping what is said to preserve accuracy. Following that, they fill in needed information through research at libraries, public offices, businesses, or whatever agency is appropriate.

Applying analytical skills, reporters always attempt to provide some explanation of the happening and ascertain the who, what, where, why, when, and how of each story. Diligence must be given to verifying all facts and names. Once all of this is accomplished, the article must be organized and written in a cohesive, interesting, easy-to-understand, fair-minded manner, keeping in mind the writing style of the particular newspaper. Deadlines constantly loom and reporters must always pay heed. An article that is not ready on time may be deemed worthless.

General assignment reporters may cover any and all types of stories, including anything from a local school board meeting, to a murder trial, to a human interest story about a child recovering from a hit-and-run accident. Other reporters may be assigned to particular geographical areas (beats), bureaus, or specific topical beats, such as sports, entertainment, or business. Those with backgrounds in particular areas may be assigned fields such as medicine, education, law, or politics. Beat reporters normally generate stories on their own, whereas assignments for general assignment reporters may stem from editors, a tip from a source, press releases, wire service stories, or the reporter's own curiosity and "nose for news."

Depending on the size and location of the paper, reporters may be expected to take photos, lay out pages, write headlines, or even perform office duties. At a large newspaper, new employees may start as news assistants, verifying information for the more established reporters. Smaller papers are more likely to give reporting assignments right away. New "recruits" may also be called upon to file, clip articles, answer phones, sell subscriptions, seek advertisements, rewrite press releases, and write obituaries and other short items. Then they may move to research, reporting, and writing.

The reporter's workplace can be both indoor and outdoor, providing a mixed environment for those who enjoy moving about. In some cases, travel is necessary. This is particularly true for correspondents typically employed by a newspaper in one area but "stationed" in another in order to provide a continuous stream of news from that location. A correspondent may work for a New York paper, for example, and live in England as a London correspondent. Both reporters and correspondents may face an element of danger, particularly when checking out on-the-scene disasters, such as floods, bombings, or armed conflicts.

Reporting can be an all-encompassing career choice. News events happen at any moment, and reporters must be ready to cover breaking stories. Thus, they may find themselves putting in a considerable number of hours; certainly a minimum of a five-day week with eight-hour days. They may not be nine-to-five days either. Because of deadlines, the newspaper business is often a 24-hour, seven-day-a-week enterprise. But there are rewards, one of which is to see your story in print with your name attached to it. Bylines, as they are called, make reporters real people and rescue them from anonymity.

In terms of financial rewards, the U.S. Department of Labor reported in the May 1992 *Occupational Outlook* that reporters and correspondents have an average minimum salary of approximately $22,000. The outlook for the future is that most job openings will result from replacing reporters who leave this occupation, making the competition for jobs very keen.

INVESTIGATIVE JOURNALISTS

Of course, investigative journalists are reporters, but they don't just report the news; they are often the ones to find and uncover the news. They may spend days, weeks, or even months delving into a particular story, and little by little they put the pieces of the puzzle together. They must know how to dig further and further to get facts that may be buried. They must have top-notch interviewing skills that put people at ease and get them to divulge details. With the often sensational stories or exposes they may work on, it is especially vital for them to substantiate their evidence before they give any information to the public. In order to be truly successful they must have a "Sherlock Holmes" type of investigative spirit.

COLUMNISTS

Columnists have the luxury of writing about topics that are deeply important to them. They are allowed to express their own opinions without worrying about presenting a balanced viewpoint. As a result, their columns usually contain a mixture of news facts interspersed with interpretation and comments.

The columns may be placed in the opinion or editorial sections or in a special place in the newspaper so readers know where to locate it. Columnists on large newspapers often sell their columns to other newspapers via syndication.

Today, with hundreds of syndicates in existence, publishers are offered a wide choice of columns. This enhances the editorial content of newspapers and provides a much larger audience for the columnist. For instance, syndicated columnist Deborah Mathis's work is seen in over 80 papers nationwide. Robin Abcarian, winner of the 1993 Pulitzer Prize for commentary, is a syndicated columnist at the *Los Angeles Times*, the country's largest paper. Betsy Hart has a weekly column that is distributed to over 350 newspapers, including the *San Diego Union* and the *St. Louis Dispatch*. Ann Quindlen, 1992 winner of the Pulitzer Prize for commentary, is a popular syndicated columnist at the *New York Times*, which has won the greatest number of Pulitzer Prizes (65). The *Guinness Book of World Records* lists Ann Landers, whose column appears in over 1,200 newspapers, as being the most syndicated columnist.

EDITORIAL WRITERS

Similar to columnists, editorial writers are able to express their own opinions without necessarily presenting both points of view. Printed on the editorial page, readers know that these articles are opinion pieces. Subjects usually covered in editorial articles include social issues (such as homelessness), education, politics, local and global problems, and just about anything else the editors feel is important to discuss and of interest to readers.

PHOTOJOURNALISTS AND NEWS CAMERAPERSONS

Photojournalists are talented individuals who can make pictures tell a story. Instead of using words on paper as reporters do, they use cameras. Good photojournalists have a knack for recognizing the human element that is necessary to produce high-caliber work. They understand that it is the relationship between individuals and events that is important, not necessarily the event itself.

Newspapers have been publishing photographs for over 100 years, and, until a few decades ago, photojournalists were simply people with cameras who situated themselves in the middle of a catastrophe ready to take pictures. Today's photojournalist is likely to be a college graduate, often with a degree in journalism or a related field. He or she has the artistic talent necessary to implement proper balance, visual attractiveness, and harmony along with the proficiency to use the necessary camera equipment.

As is true with print reporters, photojournalists often begin their careers on smaller newspapers and move to larger ones after they have gained some experience. A photographer can move on to the position of picture editor, where he or she consults with editors about selecting photos for publication and even making photo assignments, and then on to chief photographer or graphics director.

According to the National Press Photographers Association, Inc., the national average salary for beginning photojournalists is about $250 to $300 per week, depending on the size of the newspaper and its circulation. Some of the largest daily metropolitan papers have contracts with members of the American Newspaper Guild; their people average in excess of $600 per week. The U.S. Department of Labor *Occupational Outlook* for 1992–1993 lists an average annual salary of $24,814 for photojournalists, noting that substantial variations exist depending on the particular position and length of service. It states that employment in this field is expected to grow as fast as the average for all other occupations through the year 2005.

EDITORIAL CARTOONISTS

Artistically talented individuals may choose to enter the world of editorial (political) cartoonists. Using the cartoon as an art form, they offer a light, humorous, or satiric comment on our world. Often their cartoons are caricatures or funny versions of well-known people. Usually the areas of politics, social issues, education, and moral issues are "fair game" to the editorial cartoonist. Candidates with backgrounds in journalism and political science have an excellent opportunity to enter this field.

The "tools of the trade" for cartoonists are paints, brushes, felt markers, pencils, inks, T-squares, and triangles. Their office is their drawing board where they may remain for many hours completing a task. Generally they work eight or more hours a day, perhaps even six or seven days a week, to meet their deadlines. Work cannot be completed too far in advance though, because the editorial cartoonist must be right on target with the most current news.

On a typical day, a staff cartoonist will begin by listening to and reading the morning news reports, proceed to a morning meeting, allow inspiration to strike, and spend the rest of the day working on the editorial cartoon.

In terms of payment, at the *Hartford Courant* for instance, editorial cartoons bring between $75 and $150 each. Because of the Newspaper Guild in New York City, freelance cartoonists may earn as much as $1,000. A Guild staff artist receives between $800 and $1,200 a week.

EDITORS

Serving as coordinators of all newsgathering activities, editors are a vital component of every news operation. Working with reporters, photographers, and freelance and staff writers, they are responsible for choosing, assigning, and scrutinizing copy to make sure it is ready for publication. All pieces must be checked for accuracy, grammar, spelling, and overall writing quality. Stories must contain no false statements and must be in keeping with the newspaper's general style. Headlines may need to be written, and some editors have responsibility in the layout of the publication. As editorial decisions are made, stories may be rewritten, trimmed, or lengthened; pictures are chosen; and copy may be returned to reporters or writers for further development. Combining reporters' articles, wire service stories, and syndicated columns, editors organize and prepare the final product.

Editors' specific duties and titles vary depending on the size of the paper. On a large paper, for instance, there may be a feature editor who aids in the development of human interest stories and may oversee the life-styles or some similar section. In fact, there may be a number of such editors overseeing specific areas like the sports, entertainment, business, or Sunday sections.

Editorial page editors work hard at keeping abreast of the news, deciding what position to take on particular issues on local, national, and international levels. History has taught us that a newspaper's editorial policy can influence popular opinion and have a real effect on politicians and corporate and community leaders.

The editor who assigns stories to reporters may have the title of City Editor, News Editor, or Managing Editor. The managing editor or editor-in-chief is usually at the top of the editorial hierarchy and is the one who oversees the day-to-day operation, guiding the direction he or she wishes the newspaper to take. He or she often writes several editorials each week, setting the style and tone of the newspaper. In addition, he or she may select personnel. As you can see, managing editors must possess both editorial and management skills.

Editors on small newspapers will perform a greater variety of tasks. They may undertake reporting duties, edit copy, take pictures, and, in addition, operate the areas of circulation, marketing, advertising, and production. For newspapers, particularly small ones, the distinction between editor and writer is often not clearly defined as it usually is for book publishers or large circulation magazines.

The life of an editor may well be interrupted with late-breaking news; thus, it is not uncommon for editors to work more than 40 hours a week. This may mean working at all hours if they go out to cover disasters that happen in the middle of the night.

Salaries vary considerably based on the size of the newspaper, the position, and the area of the country. For instance, Northeastern newspapers generally pay higher salaries than newspapers in the Southeast, but the cost of living is also higher. The U.S. Department of Labor *Occupational Outlook* for 1992–1993 lists $20,000 (beginning average) to $30,000 (five years of experience) to $60,000 (senior editors at large newspapers) in the category of writers and editors. It states that employment is expected to increase faster than the average for all occupations through the year 2005. However, it is expected that the competition will be keen because so many people are attracted to this field. Many job openings will occur as experienced workers transfer to other occupations or leave the labor force.

COPY EDITORS

Assisting editors are entry-level employees who may be called assistant editors, production assistants, editorial assistants, or copy editors. These assistants provide a great deal of important work. Manuscripts are read for errors in grammar, spelling, punctuation, sentence structure, and viewpoint. Copy that does not flow properly is rewritten to make it smoother and more pleasing to the reader. Facts, names, and dates are verified, and manuscripts are checked for editorial policy. Great attention is given to detail and consistency in the manuscript. Necessary rewriting is completed, and assistance is provided with the page layouts of both articles and photographs. Some assistants also compose headlines, proofread printer's galleys, and make sure copy is prepared for publication. Deadlines are always looming, so these tasks need to be performed quickly and accurately.

Most copy editors work regular hours totalling 35 to 40 hours per week. Some do work on weekends or at night to accommodate certain publications. Late-developing stories may require extra odd hours to meet necessary deadlines.

PROOFREADERS

It is the responsibility of the proofreader to compare typeset material with original manuscripts to discover any discrepancies. Proofreaders are the ones who carefully examine material that is ready to go to press and make sure there are no errors in copy or composition. They search for mistakes in spelling or punctuation, missing text, wrong page numbers, typographical errors, or incorrect typefaces. They make sure pictures are in the right place and are the proper size. If mistakes are found, they mark them with proofreaders' symbols, which instruct the typesetter where to make the corrections.

Working a 35- to 40-hour week is demanding for this kind of work, which requires long periods of close concentration. Since newspaper publishing requires constant deadlines, this may cause additional stress.

Salary rates vary. Freelance proofreaders may receive as much as $15 per hour. The U.S. Department of Labor *Occupational Outlook* for 1992–1993 projects the years from 1990 to 2005 to register a decline in the number of proofreaders.

MAJOR U.S. NEWSPAPERS

Akron Beach Journal	Akron, OH
Albany Times-Union	Albany, NY
Albuquerque Journal	Albuquerque, NM
Arizona Daily Star	Tucson, AZ
Arizona Republic	Phoenix, AZ
Arkansas Democrat Gazette	Little Rock, AR
Asbury Park Press	Neptune, NJ
Atlanta Journal/Constitution	Atlanta, GA
Austin American-Statesman	Austin, TX
Baltimore Sun	Baltimore, MD
Baton Rouge Advocate	Baton Rouge, LA
Birmingham News	Birmingham, AL
Boston Globe	Boston, MA
Boston Herald	Boston, MA
Buffalo News	Buffalo, NY
Camden Courier-Post	Cherry Hill, NJ
Charleston Gazette	Charleston, WV
Charleston Daily Mail	Charleston, WV
Charlotte Observer	Charlotte, NC
Chicago Sun-Times	Chicago, IL
Chicago Tribune	Chicago, IL
Christian Science Monitor	Boston, MA
Cincinnati Enquirer	Cincinnati, OH

Cincinnati Post	Cincinnati, OH
Cleveland Plain Dealer	Cleveland, OH
Columbia State	Columbia, SC
Columbus Dispatch	Columbus, OH
Dallas Morning News	Dallas, TX
Dayton Daily News	Dayton, OH
Denver Post	Denver, CO
Des Moines Register	Des Moines, IA
Detroit Free Press	Detroit, MI
Detroit News	Detroit, MI
Evansville Courier	Evansville, IN
Evansville Press	Evansville, IN
Flint Journal	Flint, MI
Florida Times-Union	Jacksonville, FL
Fort Lauderdale Sun-Sentinel	Ft. Lauderdale, FL
Fort Wayne Journal-Gazette	Fort Wayne, IN
Fort Worth Star-Telegram	Fort Wayne, IN
Fresno Bee	Fresno, CA
Grand Rapids Press	Grand Rapids, MI
Greensboro News and Record	Greensboro, NC
Greenville News	Greenville, SC
Greenville Piedmont	Greenville, SC
Harrisburg Patriot-News	Harrisburg, PA
Hartford Courant	Hartford, CT
Honolulu Star-Bulletin	Honolulu, HI
Houston Chronicle	Houston, TX
Houston Post	Houston, TX
Indianapolis News	Indianapolis, IN
Indianapolis Star	Indianapolis, IN
Jackson Clarion-Ledger	Jackson, MS
Kansan	Kansas City, KS
Kansas City Star	Kansas City, MO
Knoxville News-Sentinel	Knoxville, TN
Lancaster New Era	Lancaster, PA
Los Angeles Times	Los Angeles, CA
Louisville Courier-Journal	Louisville, KY
Memphis Commercial Appeal	Memphis, TN
Miami Herald	Miami, FL
Milwaukee Journal	Milwaukee, WI
Milwaukee Sentinel	Milwaukee, WI
Minneapolis Star and Tribune	Minneapolis, MN
Nashville Tennessean	Nashville, TN
Newsday	Melville, NY
Newark Star-Ledger	Newark, NJ
New Haven Register	New Haven, CT

Norfolk Ledger-Star	Norfolk, VA
Norfolk Virginian-Pilot	Norfolk, VA
Oakland Tribune	Oakland, CA
Oklahoman	Oklahoma City, OK
Omaha World-Herald	Omaha, NE
Orange County Register	Santa Ana, CA
Orlando Sentinel	Orlando, FL
Peoria Journal Star	Peoria, IL
Philadelphia Daily News	Philadelphia, PA
Philadelphia Inquirer	Philadelphia, PA
Pittsburgh Post-Gazette	Pittsburgh, PA
Pittsburgh Press	Pittsburgh, PA
Portland Oregonian	Portland, OR
Providence Journal-Bulletin	Providence, RI
Palm Beach Post	Palm Beach, FL
Raleigh News and Observer	Raleigh, NC
Record	Hackensack, NJ
Richmond Times-Dispatch	Richmond, VA
Roanoke Times and World News	Roanoke, VA
Rochester Democrat and Chronicle	Rochester, NY
Rochester Times-Union	Rochester, NY
Rocky Mountain News	Denver, CO
Sacramento Bee	Sacramento, CA
Sacramento Union	Sacramento, CA
St. Paul Pioneer Press	St. Paul, MN
St. Petersburg Times	St. Petersburg, FL
Salt Lake City Tribune	Salt Lake City, UT
San Antonio Express-News	San Antonio, TX
San Antonio Light	San Antonio, TX
San Diego Union-Tribune	San Diego, CA
San Francisco Chronicle	San Francisco, CA
San Francisco Examiner	San Francisco, CA
San Jose Mercury News	San Jose, CA
Seattle Post-Intelligencer	Seattle, WA
Seattle Times	Seattle, WA
Shreveport Times	Shreveport, AL
South Bend Tribune	South Bend, IN
Spokane Chronicle	Spokane, WA
Spokane Spokesman-Review	Spokane, WA
Springfield Union-News	Springfield, MA
Syracuse Herald-Journal	Syracuse, NY
Tacoma News-Tribune	Tacoma, WA
Tampa Tribune	Tampa, FL
The Times Picayune	News Orleans, LA
Toledo Blade	Toledo, OH

Tulsa Daily World	Tulsa, OK
The Washington Post	Washington, DC
Wichita Eagle	Wichita, KS
Wisconsin State Journal	Madison, WI
Worcester Telegram and Gazette	Worcester, MA
Youngstown Vindicator	Youngstown, OH

MAJOR CANADIAN NEWSPAPERS

Toronto Star	Toronto, Ontario
Montreal Gazette	Montreal, Quebec
Ottawa Citizen	Ottawa, Ontario
Hamilton, Ontario *Spectator*	Hamilton, Ontario
Toronto Globe and Mail	Toronto, Ontario
Windsor, Ontario *Star*	Windsor, Ontario
London, Ontario *Free Press*	London, Ontario
Brantford, Ontario *Expositor*	Brantford, Ontario
North Bay, Ontario *Nugget*	North Bay, Ontario
Oshawa, Ontario *Times*	Oshawa, Ontario

A CLOSER LOOK AT.......

Carol Goddard
Journalist, Editor/Bureau Chief, Bannockburn Group, Pioneer Press Newspapers, Illinois

How did you get into this area?

A family member, who happened to be a sports writer, got me started in this business. About the time Title IX was passed, schools were scrambling to organize sports for their females. I ended up being "volunteered" for the girls' sports beat at our local newspaper. I was numb but had an English degree and, being an avid sports fan and voracious newspaper reader, I thought it might be fun.

Tell us about your first story.

I'll never forget my first story. The family member who could have helped me was out of town, so I had to do the reporting and writing on my own. I carefully crafted my words and peppered the stories with what I was sure were brilliant quotes. When he returned, I couldn't wait to show him what talent he had unwittingly tapped. I'll never forget what happened. He read the stories quietly for a long time without saying a word. Then he said, "Well, I think we can work together on this."

I was crushed. But, of course, I quickly realized that there was a lot more to newspaper reporting and writing than I had ever realized. After that, I took several journalism courses and read a number of good newspaper writers (a good way to learn about quality writing). And I was edited heavily and fully by my family member. I always encouraged him to be really tough on me, because that was the most effective teacher for me. Of course, that meant rewriting, rewriting, and more rewriting! I see quite a bit of sloppy writing and editing today, and it bothers me that our standards have relaxed so much.

What was the next step?

After that, I volunteered to take on other assignments. Both my children were in school then, so I asked for the education beat. I asked a lot of questions in the beginning, but once I understood how the system worked, it was easy to make the intricacies of the school board meaningful for my readers. By the way, this should be a cardinal rule for every journalist. You can't really write about something if you don't understand what you're talking about.

My school beat coverage made me realize that I truly liked newspaper reporting, and I asked to be considered for a full-time position if one should ever open up there. It did, and I was hired. Within three years, I was named Managing Editor.

A few years later, I was recruited by Pioneer Press and assumed the managing editor position in Oak Park, one of the company's most important communities. Going from a small, family-run operation to a large corporation was quite a shock, but I learned a great deal in the first few years thanks to a terrific editor who demanded excellence. Four years later, I was promoted to editor of one of the company's five bureaus (at the time) and since then have worked as the editor for two other bureaus. I currently hold the title of Editor/Bureau Chief for the Bannockburn Group, which includes 11 newspapers in the eastern part of Lake County, Illinois.

What are your responsibilities?

I am responsible for the news, features, photography, and sports coverage of these newspapers. Six editors report directly to me. I direct some projects, attend numerous meetings, write many reports, and try to ensure that every member of the Bannockburn editorial staff is working up to his or her potential. Doing that is hard to quantify. But our group wins its share of company and national newspaper awards, so it must be working.

What's the best part of all of this?

The best part of working in this field is the unpredictability. News is never the same in one week or one community. There's an incredible feeling of accomplishment when a complicated report all comes together and our readers are better informed for having read it. We all still get a wonderful rush when the paper is delivered and we can point to it and say, "I did that." Actually that was one of the hardest transitions for me—when I went from being a managing editor with responsibilities for a paper that I could point to each week as mine, and when I became an editor who was charged with the less quantifiable job of adding depth to the paper.

What's the worst part of the job?

The worst part of this job is when you run out of time. We are always pushing the clock, trying to get one more interview, one more quote, one more fact that will really make the story come alive. Another "worst" is seeing a mistake in the paper, from a misspelling to an error to a missing page.

What is your best advice?

My recommendation would be to become a specialist. Also, be sure you have a good fix on what it is you want to do.

Reporters have a great deal of knowledge they have to master. And as the world becomes more complicated, many staff writers are focusing their energies on specific areas: the environment, courts, schools, taxation, business, etc. They start as generalists but work into a specialist slot. I would encourage anyone starting out to get a journalism degree and also focus on a strong minor to nail down some type of specialty. Another possibility is to channel your energies into an area once you get a job.

Anyone interested in journalism should spend time figuring out what he or she wants to be: a top editor or a top reporter. Too many really first-class reporters are lured into becoming editors when what they really excel at is the reporting and writing. So they're promoted and they're miserable. Part of the learning process for each new newspaper employee ought to include time spent figuring out what area of the newspaper most appeals to him or her. If it's the editorial end, which facet—managing, editing, or reporting? Once you know this, you can direct your work into the area best suited for you.

A CLOSER LOOK AT.......

Fredric N. Tulsky
Investigative Reporter, Investigative Editor,
Center for Investigative Reporting

How did you enter the area of investigative reporting?

For as long as I can remember, I wanted to be a newspaper reporter.

I grew up on newspapers. As a boy, I can remember the excitement of running outside early each morning to gather the morning papers and check the sports scores; and then, again to read the afternoon paper each day after school.

By high school, I became managing editor of the newspaper and subsequently attended college at the University of Missouri School of Journalism.

For the grand sum of $120 per week, I landed my first job as an intern for the Saginaw, Michigan *News*. After graduation, I returned to the paper as City Hall reporter, and then went where the opportunities were: to Port Huron, Michigan; Jackson, Mississippi; Los Angeles, and then to the *Philadelphia Inquirer*, where I spent 14 years before becoming managing editor of the Center for Investigative Reporting last July.

What do you think is the appeal of investigative reporting?

To me, what makes journalism exciting is uncovering information that no one else has found. I take great pride in reporting; democracy means nothing if people are not informed.

I guess I see investigative reporting as doing just that—uncovering information about people and institutions of power that had been unknown (often because someone has been hiding the information).

Over the years, I have worked on many investigative projects, often alone and many times with at least one partner. The advantage of working with someone is that, on a long project, it is great to have someone to discuss the project with, to keep your sanity. Such projects often take anywhere from a few weeks to many months. The formula is usually the same: having an idea and using public records and people to document the idea.

To me, what differentiates a good story from a great story is showing a pattern, for instance, one of abuse. If a policeman beats someone, that is a good newspaper story. But if the reporter checks the internal affairs records, court records, and other available sources and finds that the policeman has beaten five people over the years, than a good story becomes a great story.

One example is a story I did in Philadelphia about defense attorneys who had made a practice of testifying, after their clients were convicted, that the client deserved a new trial because they themselves had performed so poorly. The first time I saw it happen, I was shocked. I was sitting in a small courtroom in a remote part of City Hall when the testimony occurred. I was there just to watch what happened, on the theory that the most likely place that a reporter can find news is the place where no reporters go. After hearing this attorney testify about his failures, I was determined to find out if this was some fluke or part of a larger pattern. I spent weeks talking to other attorneys to see if they had seen anything like it. Slowly but surely, I found one case here and one case there. (Unlike most stories, there was no place to go look up "times attorneys testified that they committed gross errors.") I then spent months documenting the anecdotes through court records and interviews.

What personal qualities do you think are necessary for investigative reporters?

I think the ingredients for an investigative reporter are simple: persistence, passion, and care. You have to be willing to spend weeks going through records and prepared to find nothing. In looking for documentation, there is no need to behave badly. In fact, I believe people are more willing to help someone who is well behaved.

What's the best part of the job?

The best part of the work is that moment when you discover that you have found something newsworthy that has not come to the public's attention beforehand.

Another one of the great things about the work is that it's always different. As a reporter, I would spend most of my time either on the telephone or out of the office, talking to people and going through records. I would either be pursuing a particular story or checking in with my steady diet of sources to see what new issues there were for me.

What's the worst part of the job?

The worst part is the weeks it takes, chasing dead ends, slogging through records, to get to that point. Equally bad is going to talk to someone whom you know will be the subject of negative publicity, and making sure that you have given him or her a full opportunity to tell his or her side.

How is your new position different from what you've been used to?

As an editor, the biggest single difference that I have found so far is the need to be able to pay attention, on any given day, to the stories that eight different reporters are working on—and each wants to talk about. It is a major difference, since as a reporter I was generally given the luxury of focusing on one story at a time, with a single-mindedness of purpose. But I look upon my new position as a welcome and most worthwhile challenge.

Fredric N. Tulsky is the recipient of many awards, most notably a Pulitzer Prize for investigative reporting in 1987. Other distinctions include a National Headliners Award for public service in 1987; a bronze medallion, SDX-SPJ for general reporting in 1977; the Heywood Broun Award, writing on behalf of the underpriviledged in 1977; grand prize, Robert F. Kennedy Journalism Award, writing on behalf of the disadvantaged in 1978; Associated Press Managing Editors, public service award, 1978; and the Gavel Award from the American Bar Association in 1978 and 1988. To add to his expertise, Tulsky earned a law degree from Temple University School of Law in 1984 and was awarded a Nieman fellowship at Harvard University, 1988–1989.

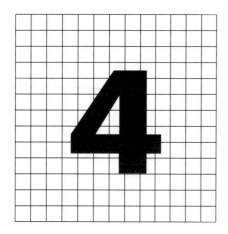

MAGAZINE PUBLISHING

Good writing is supposed to evoke sensation in the reader—
not the fact that it's raining, but the feeling of being rained
upon."

—E.L. Doctorow

Tropical Fish Hobbyist, Parents, Good Housekeeping, Career World, Red-book, Sports Illustrated, North Shore, True West, Self, Tennis, Cosmopolitan, Parade, Dog Fancy, Modern Maturity, U.S. News and World Report, People, Mac World, The National Jewish Monthly, Seventeen—The list goes on and on. No matter how old you are, no matter where you live, no matter what your profession is, no matter what your interests are, magazines offer a wide array of material that is perceptive, pleasurable, and purposeful.

Because newspapers must appeal to large numbers of people, the variety of topics that can be covered in detail is limited. Books take a lengthy period of time (generally a minimum of one year) to be written and published; thus, the information contained within may be dated. Even television cannot regularly offer us the most up-to-date information on our favorite hobby at the precise moment we are interested in exploring the topic (even with cable television and video cassette recorders). Magazines give us the luxury to explore all the subjects that are most important to us—anything from doll collecting to self-defense to bird watching—at precisely the moment we wish to do so.

According to the American Society of Magazine Editors (Magazine Publishers of America), a typical American adult purchases 36 magazines a year. This figure represents a 20 percent increase over the past ten years. According to Media Distribution Services (Associated Release Service, Inc., Chicago, IL, 1993), over 156 million adults aged eighteen and older read one or more magazines each month.

The 1993 *Guinness Book of World Records* reports that in the 41 basic international editions of *Reader's Digest* 28.5 million copies are circulated in 17 languages each month. The peak circulation of any weekly periodical was reached by *TV Guide,* which became the first magazine to sell a billion copies in one year (1974). Currently, the world's highest-circulation magazine is *Modern Maturity,* a bimonthly publication for the 50 plus generation. The *Guinness Book of World Records* lists the magazine's circulation (as of March 1992) as 22.45 million.

While it is true that every year hundreds of magazines cease publishing, even more are launched. Newsstands are filled with a diversity of offerings, but many more, literally thousands, are handled through subscriptions that go directly to the buyer's home.

Magazines are most commonly divided into two groups: consumer magazines, which are designed to appeal to mass audiences, and magazines written for trade, technical, and professional audiences.

The following is a sampling of the large number of areas included in the consumer magazine group: (business and finance) *Barron's, Forbes,* and *Money;* (home and garden) *American Horticulturist, Better Homes and Gardens,* and *Canadian Workshop;* (juvenile) *Children's Digest, Humpty Dumpty, Highlights for Children,* and *Jack and Jill;* (mystery) *Alfred Hitchcock's Mystery Magazine* and *Ellery Queen's Mystery Magazine;* (politics and world affairs) *National Review, Newsweek, The Nation,* and *Freedom;* and (science) *Popular Science, Omni,* and *Astronomy.*

Trade, technical, and professional journals also include a large number of subject areas, including the following: (Advertising, marketing, and public relations) *Imprint, Sales and Marketing Manager Canada,* and *More Business;* (Journalism and Writing) *Canadian Author, Editor and Publisher,* and *Freelance Writer's Report;* (Law) *American Bar Association Journal, Student Lawyer,* and *The National Law Journal;* and (printing) *Canadian Printer, Screen Printing,* and *Print and Graphics.*

THE EDITORIAL STAFF

Though there is great diversity among magazines, a number of factors are common to all of them. One is that on magazines the word *story* refers to both nonfiction and fiction articles, *pictures* include all visual representations, and *layouts* are diagrams of how all material will be placed on a page. A second common factor is that magazines are expected to appear at regular intervals—whether weekly, monthly, bimonthly, quarterly, annually, or biannually. Based on this fact, the publisher and the editorial staff work together to create an editorial schedule.

Staffs for magazines vary greatly depending on the kind, frequency, and size of the publication. However, most magazine organizations consist of a publisher, an exective editor or editor-in-chief, a managing editor, a senior editor, associate or assistant editors, staff writers, copy editors, editorial assistants, (possibly) fact checkers, and proofreaders.

Not every publishing company uses the same title for people who perform the same duties. Generally, though, the *publisher* is the individual who is responsible for all aspects of the publication.

Four

The *executive editor's* job may be mainly administrative, involving him or her with the day-to-day operation of the enterprise in addition to scheduling. Through essays or other opinion pieces, he or she may express the viewpoints of the magazine.

The *managing editor* usually guides and coordinates all the manuscripts and oversees the physical production of the master pages for each issue, making sure all deadlines are met. He or she is responsible for supervising other editors, staff writers, and freelancers, and possibly for working on some writing and editing projects of his or her own.

A magazine's editorial hierarchy may include *senior editors* and if so, associate and assistant editors will report to them.

Some editors are specialists in a particular area, such as beauty, home furnishings, or fashion, or they may be experts with financial, scientific, political, or medical backgrounds. In this capacity, they may do major research projects and possibly travel to conduct interviews or visit pertinent sites. Editors' titles may describe their specialty: home furnishings editor, science editor, and so forth. Magazines may also have nonfiction or fiction editors who deal only with those categories. Some magazines use *contributing editors* who are not on staff at the magazine's offices. These editors are responsible for either coming up with ideas for articles and looking for other authors to write the pieces or, in some cases, writing the pieces themselves. These individuals are often former staff employees of the magazine.

Regardless of job titles, most editors are involved in three important aspects of magazine production: (1) the creation of article ideas and themes for particular issues; (2) deciding on the stories they will tell either by selecting from the large numbers of articles that are sent in by freelancers or by assigning staff writers or other authors to write them; and (3) making sure the copy is properly edited. The latter may require revising, writing captions and titles, checking for proper article length and making adjustments as needed, verifying factual material, and reviewing galleys and page proofs. The smaller the magazine, the more likely it is that each individual performs a multitude of tasks, just as with a small newspaper. In this case, an editor might actually write articles and perform editing and even copy editing tasks. Further, editors are responsible for planning the visual part of the story. They must choose the photographs, pictures, or artwork to accompany each piece. In this area, they work closely with the art and production departments.

Photojournalists are an important asset to many magazines, just as they are to newspapers. Most magazines have their own professional photojournalists, but freelance photographers are also used.

Editorial assistants, or junior editors, perform research and office duties, set up photography sessions, cover industry events, type manuscripts, send contracts to writers, respond to letters, and possibly screen manuscripts that are sent to the editors from freelancers.

Once an editor is satisfied with a manuscript, it goes to a *copy editor* who, just as on newspapers, edits the copy for spelling, grammar, punctuation, clarity of thought, words, and style.

Magazine *proofreaders* perform the same tasks as newspaper proofreaders by examining galleys and page proofs before they go to press to make sure everything is the same as the original manuscript.

Editorial conferences are an integral part of the efficient operations of a magazine. At a prescribed time, all editorial staff members meet to brainstorm and discuss forthcoming issues and make decisions about what articles will be used. Overall, the content of magazines is overwhelmingly nonfiction; in fact, a large number of magazines don't publish any fiction at all.

Much editorial planning is carried on months in advance because of the volume of decisions needed for a magazine to maintain its high editorial quality and visual appeal while keeping its target audience and deadlines in mind.

SALARY AND EMPLOYMENT OUTLOOK

According to the Dow Jones Newspaper Fund, beginning salaries for writers and editorial assistants averaged $20,000 per year in 1990. Writers and editors working for the federal government averaged $35,635 in 1991.

The 1992–1993 edition of the *Occupation Outlook Handbook* states that employment for salaried magazine writers and editors is expected to increase along with growing demand for the publications. There will, however, be keen competition for all available positions. Opportunities will be best with business, trade, and technical publications.

A CLOSER LOOK AT.......

Timothy M. Clancy
Managing Editor, CASS Recruitment Publications

Tell us about your entrance into this field.

My entry into the journalism field was more happenstance than calculation. I was not interested in journalism in high school, though my writing always earned high marks. I originally planned to pursue a degree in optometry or psychology. During the summer between my freshman and sophomore years in college, I noticed that most of my friends were on the school newspaper. I decided to take some journalism classes and see what my friends were attracted to. Before I knew it, I was news editor and the following semester, I was named executive editor! It seems that I had found my niche. Suddenly the calculus and pre-med classes weren't nearly as exciting as being a *reporter*.

But as naive as I was, I realized that the chances of making much money as a reporter were rather slim. So I elected to take a public relations option with my journalism degree, as well as several marketing classes. I planned to get into some sort of corporate communications environment, as opposed to "hard" journalism.

Unfortunately, when I was in college, there were very few internships available for public relations students and fewer still on-campus interviews for journalism majors seeking professional employment. So while the high-tech firms were battling in the college placement office for engineers and computer scientists, we liberal arts types had a much harder time locating potential employers. Had I known then what I do now (as far as implementing your own job search plan), I probably would have secured a position faster. After sending out many resumes and cover letters, I received only one interview offer, for a management trainee position at a mid-level department store chain. I went to the interview and was so confident that I was going to get the job that I immediately rewarded myself by going on a little shopping spree at Saks Fifth Avenue in Beverly Hills. Well, I didn't get the job, but I still have the navy pin-striped Adolfo suit!

Just when I thought my future had literally gone to the dogs (working in a pet store), I received a phone call from Carcer Research Systems, a company that I had applied to for a part-time proofreader position two years earlier. They had kept my resume on file and called me back for an interview—this time for a permanent full-time editorial position. I got the job and entered the world of journalism.

Tell us about your present responsibilities.

Since the company is small in terms of number of employees, my responsibilities are varied. On a given day I may have to talk to many placement professionals at the colleges for which we publish career materials; edit an original article; work with the graphic designer on color selection for a brochure, magazine cover, or article layout; argue with a marketing person over the wording of a promotion piece, review a pre-press blueline proof, help a job seeker locate career information (phone calls of this nature are directed to me); administer a proofreading test; and conduct a job interview for a temporary position.

What are the best and worst aspects of your position?

I guess that's what I like best about this position; there's enough variety to keep it interesting. More importantly, though, is its rewarding nature since I am able to provide quality publications (free of charge to either schools or students) to many of the top schools in the country. Each *Placement Manual* is unique to its respective university and paid for by recruitment ads from companies that are seeking new grads. I get a lot of phone calls and letters from the placement directors at these schools telling me how much they appreciate what we are able to do for them. That feels really good, especially after working long hours during the main production cycle in the spring and summer.

One down side to this kind of position is that there are times when the stress level is very high; I must juggle many projects at one time, deal with emotions that accompany a heavy workload, and watch a pile of paperwork grow to the size of a small city.

How would you advise those considering a career in this field?

I would tell those interested in a publishing career to keep abreast of the changing technology of electronic publishing. Don't accept your first position with a company that does things "the old way" with conventional typesetting and mechanical paste-up (amazingly there are still companies that are in the technological Dark Ages). Try to get enough knowledge of desktop publishing so that you can interface effectively with designers/art directors/typographers. If there's a downside to the new technology, it's that some of the smaller companies are using their editors as designers, requiring them to do the actual layout and design, rather than hiring art directors. The net result is that there's a lot of amateurish and/or hackneyed desktop publishing happening. Find a company that is utilizing the new technology to its fullest—to enhance the final product, rather than using it to cut corners. It's good to get cross-trained in other areas, but in most cases, an editor/designer is probably neither a great editor nor a great designer. What I'm saying is: Develop your expertise in your career discipline and then enhance your marketability by developing a working knowledge of peripheral disciplines. In my case, it means focusing on editorial skills, but also understanding college/employer relations, typography/design, personnel matters, and the actual printing process.

Timothy J. Clancy oversees the editorial production of 150 plus annual and bimonthly career development publications for college/university students and minority professionals. He is also responsible for the hands-on editing of approximately 50 *College Placement Manuals* as well as nine annual minority *Career Development Guides* and the EEO *Bimonthly Magazine.*

A CLOSER LOOK AT.......

Mary Haley
Managing Editor, Chicago Parent

Tell us about your career history.

My work history falls into three fairly distinct parts and forms, I like to think, some kind of a logical progression. I worked for ten years as an elementary school teacher for the Archdiocese of Chicago, teaching fourth through eighth grades. After that, I accepted a position with Scott Foresman, a publisher of educational materials. At the time, the company was hiring a number of former teachers in the hopes that they could provide realistic information from the "front lines" to use in the development of their various products.

During my three years at Scott Foresman, I worked on a reading series for students with special needs. It was there that I had my first editing experience in an intensive, hands-on environment. We were responsible for everything from selecting and developing content material to tracking skills presentations, adjusting readability levels, assigning and reviewing freelance materials, and reviewing artwork. It was a trial-by-fire experience and a tremendous opportunity to learn first-hand what goes into taking a project from the idea stage to the presses.

In 1980, my husband Dan put together a group of investors and launched *Wednesday Journal,* a locally owned community newspaper in Oak Park. By 1984, the *Journal* was getting its feet on the ground, but the position of feature editor had turned over several times in less than a year. Dan was looking for someone who could bring stability to the position, and I suggested that I might be that person. We have been working together ever since (this could be the subject of another book). I worked as feature editor for the *Journal* for the next six years, developing story ideas and editing copy, working with freelance writers and photographers, and in the early years, designing my own pages.

Wednesday Journal, Inc. was looking for an expansion opportunity in 1990 when *Chicago Parent* became available. Following the purchase of *Chicago Parent,* I became managing editor.

My educational background includes a Bachelor of Arts degree in English and a master's degree in English from the University of Minnesota. I think a degree in journalism can provide a valuable grounding for someone entering the field. I took an indirect route and learned by doing (the precept of the educational master, John Dewey), perhaps not the easiest approach. But for me, being here is something that evolved rather than a goal that I set early for myself.

Tell us about your life as managing editor of Chicago Parent.

It is an editor's responsibility to have a vision of where a publication is going and to provide it with a distinctive tone. The publishing cycle determines the day-to-day experiences of an editor. Since *Chicago Parent* is a monthly publication, I typically find myself spending two weeks on short- and long-range planning and two weeks on editing and laying out the current issue.

Feature stories are planned out and assigned two to three months in advance. Most stories and regular features are assigned to freelance writers, but occasionally an unsolicited manuscript may be included (all must be read). We have a number of authors who write for us on a regular basis, but it is also important to continually find new voices for the publication. Photos and illustrations are usually assigned a month in advance of publication, as is the cover photo. Editing is done a week in advance of the production cycle. Headlines are written in collaboration with the page layout designer before pages are designed. On deadline day, all pages are reviewed as page assembly is completed.

In addition, I develop a yearly editorial budget and provide the financial manager with monthly totals as well as information on payments to be made to writers, illustrators, and photographers.

And, of course, there is the mail. Opening it can be both the most interesting and the most routine part of the day. But one thing is certain—we're never short on volume.

What's the best part of your job?

For me, the best part about working for *Chicago Parent* is that it allows me to combine two great interests, children and editorial work. It's tremendously rewarding to think that we could have a positive impact on the quality of children's lives, while providing their parents with information, support, and encouragement.

What's the worst part of your job?

The worst part, I suppose, is the unrelenting nature of deadlines. But you have to learn early to live with them or you've chosen the wrong career.

What do you look for in a prospective employee?

A background in journalism provides a realistic preparation for the job. But beyond professional preparation I would look for a person who has a high energy level and is willing to commit to hard work, is attentive to detail and likes to delve into a topic or project, is widely read and fundamentally interested in the world around [him or] her, has a positive nature, and is able to work well with people.

A CLOSER LOOK AT.......

Gigi Berman
Reader Services Editor, *Parents Magazine*

Tell us how you entered the world of publishing.

I worked at a local weekly newspaper and also started my own newspaper for college-bound students. It was funded by local advertising and actually did quite well; but not well enough.

In 1988, I began my career at *Parents Magazine* as a secretary. From there, I moved up to fact checking, the beginning of the editorial track.

Fact checkers go over all new work before it goes to a copy editor; even to the point of verifying all information and calling the interviewees to verify the quotes. It's a very laborious task, but it teaches you the important lesson of research and accuracy. People often remain at this level for two or three years, but I was lucky and after a few months there was an opening in the "Letters to the Editor" page, and I got the job in 1990.

An important part of my position as reader services editor is to read the thousands of letters *Parents Magazine* receives each week. After organizing them, I write reports based on the information I have gleaned from them. Then I discuss this input with the editor-in-chief. This is important because we make a genuine effort to give our readers what they want and sincerely encourage a dialogue with them. In fact, a new section was initiated because readers were writing in seeking help about different issues. Based on this, we developed the "Can You Help? section, which I edit each month. Typical problems (such as a mother who wrote in saying she was lonely) are featured, and people respond with suggestions to improve the situation.

I also instituted a third section called "Your Ideas" and an interoffice reader mail report to let other employees at *Parents Magazine* know what readers are thinking and feeling.

One of my other responsibilities is to handle reader phone calls. People really perceive us as experts and feel comfortable coming to us for answers. Callers may ask anything from, "What issue was the article on tetanus in?" to "I'm a new mother feeling a little depressed. What organization would you recommend I contact?" I often give reference and service advice.

What are your suggestions to others considering entering this field?

I'd say you need to be prepared to do everything and anything. You must be flexible and willing. Spend time studying the magazine you are considering. See what it needs. Don't be afraid to make suggestions and don't be afraid to be shot down. Take chances with new ideas; they are what keep magazines lively. If your idea isn't approved, think of others or know how to improve on the original one. One idea can change an entire career—it did for me.

What do you think is the best background for candidates to have?

The best combination is probably a Bachelor of Arts degree in liberal arts (with a major in a specific area, such as history) and a master's in Journalism, although it certainly isn't required. Even with those credentials you may well begin as a fact checker.

Make it clear from the beginning that you wish to move forward. Even if you remain in this entry level for one or two years, you should seize all opportunities to take any initiative. People do leave to move on to other jobs or places, so positions do open.

What is the best part of working in this field?

The best part of all this is that I'm doing something I like and utilizing my writing skills while helping others. It's not easy work, however. There is always much to do and I'm always having to shift gears. There's always a new season coming which requires new ideas. Things are never stagnant; there is always interest and diversity in this field to keep you creative and motivated.

A CLOSER LOOK AT.......

Judy Smith
Associate Editor, General Learning Corporation, Northbrook, Illinois

Tell us about your educational and career background.

I have a bachelor's degree from Indiana University where I majored in Textiles and Merchandising planning to pursue interior design or retail. Upon graduation, I worked for Marshall Fields for two years and then entered the world of writing! Because of my fashion background, I was hired by Evans, Inc., as a copywriter. Although I didn't have a journalism degree, I had taken creative writing and advertising courses. I worked at Evans in their in-house advertising department for ten years, writing copy for dress, sportswear, and fur ads. After taking time off to have my children, I accepted a position at General Learning Corporation as an editor.

What are your responsibilities?

I am an associate editor for *Career World* and *In Motion* magazines. *Career World* is a monthly educational publication that teachers subscribe to for their sixth- through twelfth-grade students. Once a year, the editors and consultants meet to plan the following year's schedule. We think of ideas for articles that we would like to include and fill them all in for the entire year. I then assign the articles (one month at a time, usually) to freelance writers. When the articles come in, I look to see if the writer has followed our directions. If not, I will either send the article back to the writer for a rewrite or fix it myself. Sometimes only minor editing changes are necessary (such as rearranging sentence order or rewording a phrase), but sometimes I do a fairly extensive rewrite.

I look for a variety of things in the manuscripts I receive from our writers. For instance, the introductory paragraph is especially important. If it doesn't pull the reader in immediately, forget it! Sometimes writers send in articles without a conclusion (it's amazing to me how often this happens), so I write one. Sometimes the article just drags on and on with no vitality and zip; it's just too dull and stiff and boring. I try to spice up the copy with language that is more reader friendly and conversational. I also make sure the article is aimed at our reading audience. The level of difficulty has to be appropriate and the style of writing has to be right on target for our audience. We don't want the vocabulary to be above their heads. We also want to avoid sounding stiff and textbook-like. Sometimes once we get an article, we find that it would be better, clearer, or more informative if something were added (like a sidebar). Other times, the articles are much too long. Then we work to make them shorter without sacrificing readability and substance.

What's a typical day like?

A typical day is very hectic. There's much to do and a tremendous amount to keep track of. All in one day, I work on articles that are scheduled to appear in several different months' issues. For example, I'm assigning new articles for March, receiving articles from writers that are scheduled for February, editing articles set for January, and checking and revising copy and layout for articles set to appear in November. It's impossible to keep everything straight in your mind, so we have a log book in which every article is logged at every stage.

Every day, I have lists of things that have to get done, all of them *rush*. It's hard to set priorities because everything is important. Today, as an example, I am attending a design meeting for the December issue. (In a design meeting, the editors meet with the designers and photo researchers to decide what photos and/or illustrations will be used to enhance the articles). Before the meeting, I am making last-minute phone calls to people who were supposed to have sent in photos of themselves to go along with articles in which they were interviewed or mentioned. After the meeting, I'm going to call the writers whom I would like to do our March articles. After I make the calls, I will sit down and write the assignments. In order to do this, I talk with my managing editor about how we see each article and how we want it to turn out. I also refer to my notes which were taken in the planning meeting which took place a year ago! It's a combination of remembering what we originally had in mind and how we see it now. We try to come up with a new angle on every article to give it freshness and relevancy.

During the day, I also do some of my own writing. I write "short takes," which are short blurbs that keep our readers abreast of anything that's important or interesting in the workplace. Before I can write these, I have to perform research to come up with current and useful information. Another writing responsibility I have on a regular basis is a game that appears on the back page of the magazine. I have to think of a fun activity, such as a crossword puzzle or matching game, that ties into one of the articles in that particular issue. At first, this was very difficult for me because I'm not a "game person." My mind just doesn't work that way. But over time, it's become easier and, in fact, once I come up with the idea, it's probably the most enjoyable task I do. It uses a lot of creativity and that's always fun for me.

What's the best part of your job?

The best part of my job is the opportunity to use my creative skills. I've always been happiest when I'm doing something creative; in fact, I don't think I could possibly be content in a job that wasn't. I'm willing to accept less money (editors don't make a lot of money) in order to have a feeling of fulfillment in my career. I also enjoy the fact that my job is very mentally stimulating. I'm always learning something new! There's also a good deal of personal satisfaction when you see some of your work *in print*! I feel really good when I come up with new ideas for articles or interesting people to interview. It makes me feel that I'm really making an important contribution to the magazine.

What's the worst part of the job?

As I mentioned earlier, editors are paid low salaries. The work is very hard, very demanding, and very stressful. We seem to battle deadlines constantly. There's always too much to do and not enough time to get it done.

What would you recommend to others considering a career in publishing?

Internships are a great way to expose yourself to the business and get some valuable experience. Do as much reading and writing as possible. Once on the job, seize the initiative; don't wait to be asked. And critically important: Be a team player; show that you are able and willing to work well with others.

A CLOSER LOOK AT.......

Karen Titus
Managing Editor, *North Shore Magazine*

What would you tell others about becoming an editor?

Interestingly, most of the editors I know started out in this field wanting to be writers. They loved to write; they were "people persons;" they wanted to tell stories; they wanted to change the world. And, frankly, many of them were simply shy and wanted to interact with the world behind the safety of a pen and a reporter's notebook.

What often happens, however, is that people with a burning desire to write become so good at their chosen field that they are promoted right on out of it. Lured by better money (relatively speaking, of course), an opportunity to manage others, and more power to decide what gets put into the pages of a magazine or newspaper, they become editors.

At this juncture they may be doing very little writing unless it's needed to fill a news hole at the last minute. The journalist's safe anonymity is replaced with an editor's responsibility to interact with the publisher, art directors, writers, ad sales reps, PR people, potential advertisers, and, occasionally, a reader. The stories they now tell are complicated sagas involving budgets and multiple deadlines, advertorial sections and artwork.

More importantly, editors enjoy genuine satisfaction of transforming mere ideas and questions into something solid: an entire magazine or paper that ends up in the hands, minds, and, occasionally, even the hearts of countless readers. Being involved in, and being driven crazy by, all the stages of this transformation, from making the story assignments to shaping the layout to proofing the final pages, makes this transformation that much more rewarding.

Karen Titus has served as managing editor at *North Shore Magazine* for the past three and a half years.

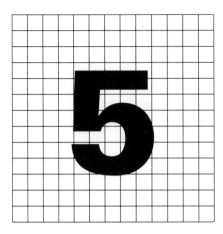

BOOK PUBLISHING

A good book is the precious life-blood of a master spirit,
embalmed and treasured up on purpose to a life beyond life.
—John Milton

Books embody the hopes and dreams of all generations. They are a living chronicle of past ages, contemporary times, and decades yet to come. In allowing us to escape from the insecurities and problems of our everyday lives, books provide information, elucidation, relaxation, and inspiration. Once we enter a book's world, we are transported somewhere else.

All books begin as ideas that may come from an author or an editor at a publishing company. If the editor at the publishing company creates the idea, he or she will seek out an appropriate author he or she feels comfortable with to write the book; generally someone who has a proven record of producing high-quality work on deadline.

If the author suggests the idea, he or she will compose an outline or table of contents and write a number of sample chapters. Working on his or her own behalf, or through the efforts of an agent, an author will approach publishing companies with manuscripts. Some publishers will want to see a completed manuscript before they will decide whether or not they will publish the book; others will decide on the basis of the sample chapters. Decisions about publishing books must be based not only on the quality of the manuscript but on its marketability. After all, what's the point of having a book published (no matter how good it is), if you don't sell many copies? Publishers cannot afford to publish books that do not sell. Because of this, editors may consult sales, marketing, and other experts to provide feedback on proposed books.

Since publishers usually specialize in specific markets, the world of books is divided into several categories. These include: trade book publishers, paperback publishers, textbook publishers, small press and university publishers, and religious presses.

There may be a number of editors on the staff of a publishing company, depending on its size. The hierarchy may vary, but usually editors stay involved in a book's progress all the way from the original assignment or acceptance of the manuscript until it is published. They are the ones who work with the author on developing the book and any other issues between the writer and the publishing company. Deadlines, set by all publishers to keep the production of books moving along at a fruitful pace, will be agreed on by writer and editor along with other contractual issues, such as advances and royalties.

TRADE BOOK PUBLISHERS

In book publishing, the term *trade books* (also called *mass market*) refers to those designed to appeal to the general population, such as mysteries, romances, biographies, and science fiction. A vast category, trade books include both fiction and nonfiction genres as well as adult and children's (or juvenile) levels.

Those entering book publishing often begin as *editorial assistants* or assistants to an editor. In this capacity they may handle correspondence, answer phones, and act as first readers for the possible thousands of manuscripts that are sent in every year by freelancers. Entry-level positions may also exist for writing copy in the advertising and publicity departments.

The next step up would be to *assistant editor.* In this position, individuals may also spend many hours reading manuscripts, create book jacket copy, and provide whatever assistance is needed by upper-level editors.

Positions up the editorial hierarchy include junior editor, associate editor, acquisitions editor, editor, senior editor, executive or managing editor (managing is usually more administrative than straight editing), associate publisher, editor-in-chief or editorial director, and president or publisher. Though *acquisitions editor* is sometimes a title given to one individual, in truth, most editors deal with aspects of acquisitions.

The *editor-in-chief, editorial director,* and/or *publisher* must be knowledgeable of both the editorial and illustrative areas and also be attuned to the business part of publishing. He or she will be in charge of the annual operating budget, working hand in hand with financial and marketing departments to formulate short- and long-range editorial projects and keep abreast of sales feasibility studies. This professional is ultimately the one responsible for how a book performs in the marketplace, its overall quality and value, and how many copies it sells. Additionally, top editors must provide a balanced book "list" that will be profitable to the company.

Every editor associated with any book may make suggestions about clarity, organization, improvement in writing style or content, or how to make the book more interesting. Sometimes the term *line editing* is used to describe the process of carefully scrutinizing the manuscript for content, style, mechanics, and accuracy. If there is a substantial amount of work required or desired, the manuscript may be sent back to the writer for revision.

Once editors finish with manuscripts, they are usually passed to *copy editors,* and then *proofreaders* will compare the finished copy with the printed proof, indicating where there are any discrepancies in style, missing material, or typographical errors.

It is important that editors handle the flow of edited manuscripts, galleys, and page proofs to and from the authors and production department. If the department or company is a small one, a single editor and his or her assistant may be responsible for these tasks.

CHILDREN'S BOOK PUBLISHERS

The concept of treating children's books (everything from picturebooks to teen-age fiction or nonfiction) as a separate entity is a relatively new one in the world of book publishing. MacMillan Company became the first publisher to set up a separate department specifically for children's books shortly after World War I.

Today, children's publishing is an important segment of overall book publishing. In 1991, almost 5,200 children's books were published out of approximately 47,000 books published in total. In 1990, total U.S. publishing dollars amounted to approximately $3.77 billion with juvenile books accounting for $987 million.*

Although children's book publishing is similar to adult trade publishing, there are some important distinctions. One lies in the additional importance given to the visual aspect of children's books. This makes it more crucial for children's book editors to have excellent visual acuities. They will work more closely with art directors, who will also play a more important role in children's publishing than they would in the adult trade segment.

Another difference between children's and adult books is in the area of marketing. Adult books are generally sold through bookstores, whereas a high percentage, perhaps 70 percent, of children's hardcover book sales come from school and public libraries. Understandably, the percentage is greater for nonfiction than for picturebooks, which do fairly well in bookstores.

Based on figures provided by *Publishers Weekly,* the leading categories in production for books released in the United States in 1991 were:

1. Economics, Sociology
2. Juvenile
3. Fiction
4. Medicine
5. Science
6. History
7. Technology

*James Cross Giblin, *Book Publishing Career Directory,* (Hawthorne, N.J.: Careers Press, 1993).

8. Religion
9. Literature
10. Biography

Most publishers create schedules that allow children's books to come out in the spring and fall, to coincide roughly with the school semesters.

Once an editor has made the decision to publish a particular book, he or she will meet closely with production staff to determine cost estimates. Then negotiations will begin with the author or agent and illustrator, if there is one. (If not, the publishing company will provide one.) Often children's book authors and illustrators represent themselves and do not have agents. Standard royalties for children's books are usually about 10 percent, but if the book is a picture book, the author and illustrator split an equal portion with each receiving five percent.

PAPERBACK PUBLISHERS

Many trade book publishers have paperback divisions. Occasionally, they produce original manuscripts but, more often than not, they publish paperback versions of books already printed in hardcover. Sold mainly through newsstands and retail outlets, paperbacks are generally divided into two categories: mass market and trade. Mass market paperbacks are sold via local and national distributors just as magazines are. Trade paperbacks are usually sold through retail stores, including book departments of department stores, chain stores, and other types of bookstores.

The main editorial responsibilities in paperback publishing are to work with the sales department to determine titles that will bring the greatest profit. This either means choosing books already in hardcover or publishing a new manuscript. If editors decide to reprint an existing hardcover book, they work on improving the copy and developing an appealing visual approach.

Editors involved in the publication of original manuscripts need essentially the same attributes as trade editors: the ability to come up with creative ideas, to formulate topics, and to find writers to accept projects. They also search through unsolicited manuscripts and deal with literary agents and contracts.

TEXTBOOK PUBLISHERS

Textbook production is an important segment of educational publishing. Included in this field are all elementary and secondary textbooks (called el-hi or school textbooks), both in hard- and softcover; manuals; maps; and other materials. These are intended for classroom use and are sold primarily to school districts. College textbooks include hard- and softcover books, audiovisual materials, and reference books, such as dictionaries and encyclopedias.

A company may have a textbook division or publish textbooks exclusively.

National Textbook Company, publisher of this book, for instance, publishes secondary and college textbooks in addition to publishing trade books.

Because of some of the differences between textbook and trade publishers, there are some editorial differences. If a trade book does not do well, other books on the list may make up for it. But for textbook publishers, this kind of loss could be catastrophic. With one new high school textbook representing an outlay of perhaps $250,000, mistakes cannot be made.

School textbook publishing is unique in that many, many people will all be working on one project, perhaps a new science project. This generally entails creating a book for every level from kindergarten through eighth grade plus teacher's editions and ancillary materials. Curriculum specifications, accurate subject matter, and market research data, as well as a team spirit of cooperation, are all crucial to the smooth development of these projects.

At the top of the editorial hierarchy in textbook publishing are *executive editors* whose primary responsibilities are in planning and management. The editorial hierarchy may continue on to senior editors, project editors, associate editors, assistant editors, and editorial assistants. To create the text, editors often seek out additional help from various sources: specialists in the field, established authors, and freelance writers. In addition, projects must be coordinated with production editors, designers, and artists. The material always must be carefully created, edited, and proofread by project members.

Once the book is produced, a *senior,* or *project, editor* may be called upon to help with marketing the series by providing seminars and explanations of the series to sales staff or presentations at state adoption meetings, conventions, or other marketing situations.

BOOK CLUBS

A book club is a combination of a publishing organization and a retail operation; one that markets books published by other publishers. Although clubs offer a relatively small number of books compared to a bookstore, they appeal to particular segments of the population who are known to be interested in specific topics or hobbies, such as writers, mystery readers, gardeners, and music aficionados.

Book clubs get their books from publishers who mail them as manuscripts or galley proofs. The Book-of-the-Month Club, for example, receives about 5,000 book submissions a year. Submissions are read and judged by *editors* for their content and appeal, the author's credentials, and enjoyment.

Both small and large clubs generally use outside readers besides their staff editors. This is a real possibility for those trying to break into the field.

When editors decide they like a book and want to publish it, they contact the publisher's subsidiary rights department and make an offer. All of this sounds pretty routine for editors at any publishing concern. The book clubs, however, produce their version of the book, adding whatever they choose in terms of copy or visuals.

There are three main differences between trade publishing and book clubs.

1. Book club editors are considering books that have already been published, not making decisions about whether or not to publish. This saves them from having to wade through hundreds of unpublished manuscripts submitted by freelance writers.
2. Book club editors generally don't do manuscript editing.
3. Book club editors don't usually deal directly with authors or agents. But like other editors, they are responsible for the choices they made and how successfully they resulted in earning money for the company.

Once editors decide which books they will present to their club members, they must set up a schedule and produce monthly bulletins (basically magazine publications), often 15 per year. This schedule, originally devised by the Book-of-the-Month Club, is based on the 12 months plus spring, summer, and fall. Copywriters create the book descriptions to be included in the newsletter bulletins. It is very important that these are well written to make the books seem enticing. People, after all, are buying something sight unseen!

At book clubs, entry-level *editorial assistants* perform research and office tasks and read submitted manuscripts. *Copy editors* and *proofreaders* check all copy for grammar, style, punctuation, and accuracy just as they do in all areas of publishing.

SMALL PRESSES

A small press operates in pretty much the same way as a large one, except with limited projects, personnel, and money. Sometimes small presses are born as a result of an individual who decides to self-publish and then continues to add other books to his or her book list. *The Hunt for Red October,* Tom Clancy's first novel, was bought by a small press, the Naval Institute Press.

With the advent of desktop publishing, many have entered the world of small press publishing. It is now possible for a small publisher to produce a credible product for just a few thousand dollars. Desktop publishing has also shortened the length of time it takes to get a book published and made it feasible to run small printings economically.

UNIVERSITY PRESSES

University presses usually seek works that are of interest to professionals and scholars, such as scientific, medical, technical, or business books.

When an editor finds a manuscript that he or she deems worthy of printing, he has a contract drawn up with the writer and thus becomes the *sponsoring editor.* Often works are sought from college professors. Then the work will be reviewed, suggestions will be made, and the author will implement them. The editor and writer work together to improve the work. To help the sponsoring editor are *editorial assistants* and possibly a *manuscript editor.* Manuscript editors (copy editors) perform the same duties as similar positions in other fields.

RELIGIOUS PRESSES

Religious publishers focus on social and theological issues. They are organized in much the same manner as other types of publishers: Editors create ideas; choose manuscripts or writers to complete desired manuscripts; and make sure that copy is edited, copy edited, and proofread.

One important difference, though, is that the authors the editors work with are usually religious individuals, often in the clergy. They may be highly regarded for their religious work but not necessarily for their proficiency in writing. Thus, they may need more editorial help than professional writers.

SALARY AND EMPLOYMENT OUTLOOK

Starting salaries in the field of trade editorial are in the $14,000 to $18,000 range. (Source—Samuel S. Vaughan, Editor-at-large at Random House, Inc. and William Morrow, Inc.—Books Publishing Career Directory, 1993).

A CLOSER LOOK AT.......

Richard Jackson
Editor of Richard Jackson Books, an imprint of Orchard Books

The following appeared in the *Children's Book Council Features* (Newsletter) July–December issue, 1992. It is a shortened version of a speech presented to an American Booksellers Association Conference.

It clearly answers the question:

Tell us what it means to be a children's book editor.

Editors have all the fun, or at least a lot of it. If you like reading, well, editors read. Of the hundreds, sometimes thousands, of manuscripts received every year by a publishing house, maybe 1 percent are actually purchased. Early on, you learn to ask, Does this convince me? Do I care what happens to these people? Is the voice authentic? Has a young person's nature somehow caused the action? Have I read this before? These same questions pertain to a writer you've already published or to a newcomer. You must apply your own taste to everything you read.

If you like pictures, the opportunity for fun is unlimited. As an editor, you have the responsibility of choosing artists for picturebooks, illustrated stories, and probably jackets for novels.

Considerable time can go into matchmaking between words and pictures. Oddly, it often happens that the writer of a picturebook and the book's illustrator never meet, that they communicate only through the editor.

If you like therapy, editorial work will fulfill you. Much of it concerns the nurturing, interested inquiry and truth seeking that a therapist offers a patient. Writers and artists often lead isolated lives. To sign a book contract is to take on a life—not only of the book, but also of the writer or artist. It helps, in editorial work, if people interest you.

You do lots of telephoning to check up on progress, to tune in, to share a joke. It is not necessary to become a writer's best buddy, but sometimes that happens, and sometimes that's good for the work.

If you like speechmaking, there are many chances for that. For editors in some houses present the books they wish to do to publishing committees for approval before being able to issue a contract. Then, after months and months of work with the writer and illustrator, after reading the script probably nine times at least, they present those books to their firm's sales force. It's good for a book if its editor is an effective speechmaker, able to go to its heart in a few lines that can be remembered, that can make the book distinct from others.

Maybe you like negotiation. Editors negotiate contracts with writers and artists or with their agents. The key to negotiation is to be straight, realistic, and fair to both sides. You must never be jokey or cavalier about money; it's serious stuff. In a perfect world, published writers would be able to live on their work. We all know that most of them don't.

If you like writing, there's plenty of that. Maybe a two-line note to a writer you've heard of or to an artist whose work you've spotted in a gallery. A simple hello, and did you ever think of children's books? On the other hand, you might write ten pages on a book in progress. Such letters might be philosophical or very specific blueprints for revision; at best, they can thrill writers with the possibilities of their own work.

Besides letters, there is the matter of writing catalog and jacket copy. It's difficult work, capturing what you feel about a book you love. Catalog copy is written for adult readers who may not have seen the book; it should catch the tone of the piece and entice the copy reader to be interested in the book when it shows up. This is selling copy. Flap copy, on the other hand, is read by someone with book in hand, perhaps a young reader. Summaries, so useful for school book reports, rarely make effective copy, which ought to encourage a reader to flip the book open, not think he's already read it.

If you are into sex changes, it sometimes becomes an editor's work to suggest that a male character could effectively become female and to the story's advantage in the marketplace.

Editors must think always of the story's advantage, to itself and for its audience, which we know is not always its market. There are adults to consider, but should you publish for them? There are as many answers to the question as there are editors. Here are two examples.

A young writer, whose first picturebook you've published with some success, has an idea for a novel about a girl, a father, and a bridge. That's all you know.

You say to her, "Write a scene or two; get a feel for how the people sound." She tries. She hates it. You say, "Send it in anyway." You read and maybe see why she hates it (for part of your job is to intuit); the story is perhaps autobiographical and therefore limited in this early version by what actually happened. You tell her, "Forget the actual and imagine what happens. And try it in third person instead."

The young writer groans, but tries it, and after many weeks of tinkering, feels better. Something small you've said has freed her. It's often something small.

The story may be a year away from delivery. Yet from the moment of your first interest, before any contract is discussed, a book has begun to stir and shift. It is a living thing—living now between writer and editor—partly because you, as editor, are investing hope and thought in it. Note, please, that the idea came to you, not from you; the best fiction generally comes from inside writers, not from headlines you've read or notions you've had about the market. That's why questions about trends are so discouraging; trends do not account for good books. Only writers and artists do that. Working from inside themselves.

Example two is a "commissioned" project. A painter has done a large canvas for her children. One day, you catch sight of it, partly covered over, in her studio. You ask, "What's that?" And a story floods out, for it is a painting about personal history and is densely metaphoric. The painter had not thought of a book, but she knows so much and feels so much about her subject—one not often covered for children—that you suggest a book. Something begins, simply because you were there and looking.

Considering the influence they may have in the life of anyone young, there are surprisingly few children's book editors. Only a couple of hundred—with many others knocking feverishly at the doors, because the work is fascinating. To them I say: Editors have an important job besides reading, looking at pictures, copywriting and letterwriting, keeping in touch, negotiating, cajoling, goading, encouraging, turning others on to their work, and juggling maybe 50 books in progress at a time—that job is to be an optimist.

Richard Jackson is Editor of Richard Jackson Books, an imprint of Orchard Books. After beginning his career at Doubleday and Macmillan, Jackson co-founded Bradbury Press with Robert Verrone. Jackson has edited the Newbery Award-winning *The Slave Dancer* by Paula Fox; *Missing May* by

Cynthia Rylant; Paul Goble's Caldecott Medal book, *The Girl Who Loved Wild Horses;* and nine Newbery and Caldecott Honor Books. Other authors and artists he has worked with include Judy Blume, Janet Taylor Lisle, Peter Catalanotto, Stephen Gammell, and Gary Paulsen.

A CLOSER LOOK AT.......

Dorothy Haas
Children's Book Author, Editor

How did you happen to enter dual fields of editing and writing books for children?

After graduating from college as an English major, I located the ideal position for me in my hometown, Racine, Wisconsin. Hired as a summer assistant in the editorial department of Whitman Publishing Company (at the time an editing and publishing arm of a very large printer, Western Publishing), I was expected to proofread, plan pictures for children's books, and do odd jobs. With the atmosphere of children's books all around me, I decided to be challenged by writing one. (Actually, I had written children's books in high school and had received some encouragement). So, in my spare time on weekends and in the evenings, I did a picturebook about a puppy who was lost and later found with the help of a magnifying glass. Once finished, I took it to the head of the editorial department and submitted it as *Little Joe's Puppy.* To my delight, the company decided they wanted to publish the book. And to make a wonderful situation even better, they then asked if I wanted to stay on as a permanent editor. Within two months of my college graduation, I had jumped into both fields.

How did things progress after that?

I worked hard as an editor by day and seized every spare moment to write after hours. Within a few years, I had done several more books for Whitman—picture books, a collection of biographies of famous scientists, and a novelette about Sir Lancelot. And all the time I was growing, both as an editor and as a writer.

Was it helpful for you to be following dual careers?

It was helpful in that I became totally immersed in the field of children's books. I read all the classics. I went to the library and read everything there. I went to the bookstore to search out all the new books. I read everything that the well-known academics had to say on the subject of children's books. All this was advantageous because pretty soon I began to have notions of what I thought was good and what I thought lacked something.

On the other side of the coin, being an editor makes you question everything, and in writing it makes setting down a first draft a very difficult thing for me. I'm so critical I can hardly let the creative juices flow.

How would you compare editing to writing?

If you think about writing and editing as two sides of a cube, one would be opposite the other. Both are built upon a feeling for words and the expression of ideas. But though they are part of the same process, they require two entirely different sets of skills.

What would you recommend to those considering entering these fields?

I would advise that you examine yourself, your needs, your strengths, your interests. Be flexible and willing to do many things, but build on your own strengths. Don't try to be all things to all people.

There are so many different kinds of writing and editing; you need to determine what is best for you. Are you interested in sports or science? Would you feel comfortable writing for a magazine, textbook company, advertising agency, or newspaper? Find out what you're best at and then seek out a position in that area.

When you are starting out, read, read, read the kinds of things you want to write about. After reading everything out there, ask yourself some questions. Do you like the work? Do you dislike the work? Why? Then take a book you enjoyed and deface it with colored highlights by analyzing the passages you particularly liked. "Oh, here's a good passage of dialogue," you might say, or "Here's how the author got from last week to this morning." The passage of time is not easy to handle convincingly. Later, when you're having trouble showing that time has elapsed in your own story, you can look back at your marked-up book and see how the writer handled it. This practice can give you good pointers to implement in your own writing.

Novices or others who are not writers have no conception of the writer's craft. After you delve into it, you begin to assess all the skills that are necessary, and then as you gain expertise, you begin to acquire them. But no matter what level you're at, you're still learning. What you do can always be better. In fact, I believe if the new writer looks at his or her work and says, "I can make this better," he or she is already a writer, but when a neophyte looks at something and says, "Isn't this wonderful, I don't think it can be improved," I suspect that individual may never become a truly fulfilled writer.

What I am saying is, the working writer must have insight into the quality of his or her own work.

How do you know when a book is completed?

When something is right I have a gut feeling, an inner sense of "rightness," that it's completed. If something is not right, a vague feeling of "wrongness" nags somewhere at the back of my mind. It's easy to ignore that nagging little voice. I have learned to let it surface and pay attention to it. I would tell others to recognize their own nagging voice and listen to it. After working through revision, after revision, after revision, you will finally achieve your own gut feeling, that inner sense of "rightness," the feeling of satisfaction and completion which comes from knowing that the work has reached its potential and become what you want it to be.

Dorothy Haas is happy to report that she now creates children's books full time. In her 27 years as a children's book editor, she was responsible for the publication of more than 600 books. As an author, her juveniles number more than 50 books. Among the most recent are: *Burton and the Giggle Machine,* Bradbury Press (1992); *Burton's Zoom Zoom Va-Rooom Machine,* Bradbury Press (1990); *The Secret Life of Dilly McBean,* Bradbury Press (1986); and *Peanut Butter and Jelly,* a series published by Scholastic, Books 7, 8, and 9 published in 1990. Haas is listed in Gale Research's *Something About the Author Autobiography Series* (Fall 1993); Wilson's *Sixth Book of Junior Authors and Illustrators;* and Gale Research's *Something About the Author, Contemporary American Authors,* new revision series, volume 20. Reviews of her work include the following about *Burton and the Giggle Machine:* "The story develops with an undeniable sense of style and an irrepressible sense of humor" (Booklist). "...sending a powerful message that problem solving is hard work that can be both liberating and gratifying" (Kirkus). She was featured in *Book Links* January 1993 issue saluting Good Books of 1992.

A CLOSER LOOK AT.......

Mary Elise Monsell
Children's Book Author, Teacher

Describe your life as a children's book author.
Food's good and you meet interesting people

Wrigley Field was hot. But it was hotter in the bleachers. The rock hopper penguin detective Mr. Pin and his friend Maggie were sitting under the scoreboard, watching the Cubs.

—From *The Spy Who Came North From the Pole* by M. Monsell

It's great being a children's book author. I get to visit interesting places,…meet unusual people:

"You must work for the museum," said Mr. Pin.
"Yes," said the man in white. "I am a paleontologist. I study dinosaurs. I am Professor Hugo Femur."

—Mr. Pin: *The Chocolate Files* by M. Monsell

And *most* of the time, the food is quite good, with one or two exceptions…
The glass door of the case had been forced open, so the penguin detective was able to dip his wing into the case and lightly touch a chocolate egg. He preened his wing, then announced, "There is something wrong with this chocolate."

—Mr. Pin: *The Chocolate Files*

There are highs and lows as in any business. And there are uncertainties one tries to meet with an abundance of chocolate and a good part-time job:
It had been days since Mr. Pin left his home at the South Pole to be a detective in Chicago.

—*The Mysterious Cases of Mr. Pin* by M. Monsell

Tell us about a typical day.

My day begins with my family: two boys, two gerbils, two lizards. Once they are at school, I am able to write for a few hours. Sometimes I don't. When I sometimes don't, I visit schools, teach at a junior college, volunteer, or give speeches. I also write letters, edit manuscripts, return phone calls, and in general, do the business of being a writer. I write on weekends, late at night, in waiting rooms, and in grocery lines. In short, I write anywhere. I get crabby if I don't write. Mr. Pin was written at my dining room table with intermittent screen door slams and cries of "Mom!!!" punctuating my literary pursuit.

I think it has always been this way, the wanting to write part. Since I was seven, I knew I wanted to be writer, but if that didn't work, I'd be a philosopher. The less lofty goal triumphed. That success began with a somewhat haphazard approach where I randomly submitted stories to publishers. Then I decided to treat my writing as a business. I researched children's books, publishers, and made up a schedule of writing ten books and submitting each of them to ten publishers. The real success was believing I could do it. The first book in this new plan was Mr. Pin. It was accepted by the third publisher I sent it to. Today it is an IRA/CBA Children's Choice. Mr. Pin has become a series; it is published in paperback and sold in book clubs.

I find that as an artist I need to continually reassure myself, despite small victories, that what I am doing is right. It would be nice to drive a car without rust, I think. The truth is that writing for children is what I do best. I think I would be just adequate at another, less creative career. Besides, with a quick flick of a few keys, I can make any event happen or resolve, involving any number of obscure characters, such as, Orfo the Orangutan, Mort Chissel (the fossil man), Dr. Herbert Rootrot, among others.

What advice would you give to others considering this field?

There is a little insanity to this profession along with dogged hard work. I'm not sure how to best prepare oneself for the art of writing for children. I began with a degree from Northwestern's Medill School of Journalism, taught Montessori school for several years, and spent a lot of time with my two boys. But I think the best preparation is to lead a good life. Read a lot, visit places. Ask many questions. Think about things. Why do people say things which are untrue or unkind? What would happen if they didn't? How would they change? What do I wish for? What does a child wish? What do you feel when the worst thing happens? How did I feel when I lost someone in my life? How would I react as a child? What would make it better?

I draw from my own life experiences, the sorrows and joys, and how I somehow appear in the next life event, somewhat wrinkled, a little worn, but knowing more. It's really no mystery why I do what I do. I love to make children laugh and make them feel better, to tell them stories from my heart to theirs in the voices of wood turtles and penguins. You see, it's the creatures I create that do all of the thinking. I merely record what they tell me to write. And if you buy into *that* fantasy, you may have a career waiting for you writing for the most wonderful of readers: children.

Mary Elise Monsell is the author of seven children's books. Her first book, *Underwear* (Albert Whitman), was chosen favorite picturebook by the children in the state of Wisconsin. She recently earned an M.A.T. from National–Louis University and currently teaches writing and reading classes at Oakton Community College, in addition to conducting children's and teacher's workshops.

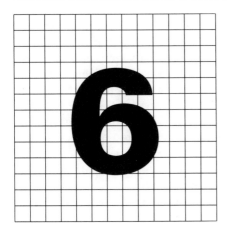

ELECTRONIC MEDIA

Good writing is a kind of skating which carries off the performer where he would not go.

—Ralph Waldo Emerson

The room is alive with the bustle of people scurrying in all directions. The clock on the wall inches its way toward five, but no one seems to notice. Suddenly a loud voice says, "Ten seconds." Some voices are quieted; others continue to be heard. "Five seconds...four...three...two...one." Suddenly there is silence. They are on the air.

The mediums of television and radio are brought to us through the erstwhile efforts of a large number of individuals performing a multitude of tasks. In most stations there are four departments: programming, sales, administration, and engineering. The news department, home of busy journalists, may be considered part of programming, or it may stand on its own as a separate entity.

NEWSROOM STAFF

The newsroom is often a flurry of activity, especially when events are breaking. Amazingly, its organization and efficiency permit the public to know what is happening at any time, day or night.

At large stations, the jobs are more specialized; at smaller stations, everyone does everything (or a lot of things). Here, generalists need to be proficient in many areas. For instance, announcers may do their own writing in addition to selling advertising.

News Desk Assistants

News desk assistants are hired to provide help for everyone in the newsroom. Their duties generally include answering phones, updating files, carrying on correspondence and other general office duties, checking facts, and tearing off incoming stories from wire services.

News Reporters

Reporters in broadcast news (also referred to as news announcers, commentators, analysts, or newscasters) operate much the way print reporters do. They too gather the elements of a news story from a variety of sources, including interviews, observation, press briefings, research, efficient use of the telephone, and leads from wire services. Reporters also decide from what perspective stories will be written (the slant), pursue follow-up stories of past events, and check out tips of news-breaking stories from the public.

At small stations, where there may be no news writers, reporters may also write the stories and deliver them on the air. At larger stations, reporters may be specialists in one area or another, for instance, health or politics. In this case, news writers work with reporters to develop stories.

Reporters may put in long, irregular hours (perhaps 12-hour days) especially when a story is developing and must continue to be followed, no matter what time it is.

News Writers

Along with the organizing and writing of broadcast news, the news writer may research background information, verify facts for stories, book guests for live interviews on news shows, and even produce some segments of news programs. He or she may also be asked to match words to video images, which demands excellent timing.

News writers may perform both writing and editing duties on news stories, commentaries, introductions, and public affairs or documentary programs produced by the news department. Often, news writers get the core information from a wire service story, then add quotes and other interesting material to round out the story. Much of the writing these professionals do is for anchorpersons and in-studio reporters.

Sportscasters

Sportscasters (also called sports directors or sports reporters) are the reporters of all news related to sports and athletic events. Performing their duties at a regularly scheduled portion of the news program, sportscasters are often former athletes, coaches, or newspaper sportswriters. Their duties are not unlike those of a general reporter except that they deal in a specialized area—sports.

At small radio or television stations, sportscasters often seek out all the sports information and news, organize it, write it, and present it on the air. At larger stations, there may be several people who all report to a sports director. Individuals may be responsible for specific sports or events.

Sportscasters go considerably beyond reporting game scores. They travel often and delve into sports-related issues, such as baseball strikes, the lives of local sports personalities, and charity events that sports figures are involved with. Sportscasters also review syndicated and wire service sports stories, choose the video footage they want to use on the air, offer play-by-play segments for television viewers, interview sports figures both on and off the air, and create and develop special sports features.

As is the case with all on-the-air performers, sportscasters must have a charismatic voice and style in order to develop a following.

Weather Reporters (Meteorologists)

Those who present the weather on camera range from highly knowledgeable meteorologists (usually in major cities) to those with less distinguished qualifications but an overall likable manner, pleasant appearance, and good verbal acuity. Local stations, major networks, cable stations, and The Weather Channel all employ them.

Responsibilities include gathering daily information about weather conditions and making the much maligned weather forecast. Data is gleaned from national satellite weather services, wire service reports, and local and regional government agencies. In larger stations they may even have their own weather equipment.

Weather reporters must have a high degree of skill in operating sophisticated weather radar systems and their associated computer graphics used to show temperature, humidity, barometric pressure, pollen count, and wind speed.

Weather reporters are always dreaming up new ways to make the visual aspects of presenting the weather more interesting and informative.

Anchors (Newscasters)

Anchors serve as the hosts or hostesses for news programs. Generally attractive and personable, they are the individuals we invite into our homes each day. It is important that anchors make viewers want to turn to their channel. After all, the same news is often being delivered on many channels at the same time. Why do people turn to one channel over another? Usually it's because of the anchor on that station. Though it is important to be appealing, the anchor's job is to inform, not to charm or win over.

At large stations, news anchors don't have to write their own stories. At smaller stations, anchors write their own material and may even act as reporters. Even at the large stations, anchors often write or rewrite some of the material. They often conduct on-camera interviews in the studio or on location and host special reports and documentary productions.

Often assigned dual roles, anchors host a particular time slot in addition to acting as on-the-scene reporters, researching stories, and doing interviews live or on tape.

News Directors

News directors are the senior executives who are in charge of everything that goes on in their news departments. The position is often more managerial than journalistic, requiring supervision of all staff.

Making all final decisions on what news will be covered and from what perspective, news directors strive to present the news completely and fairly. To that end, they edit news copy and review and approve news film and videotape footage.

News directors must have experience in all aspects of the newsroom; reporting, writing, producing, and presenting the news.

News directors' origins are always in journalism, but with today's technological progress, news directors must also be familiar with technical aspects of news gathering in addition to managing a huge budget.

They must also be knowledgeable about Federal Communications Commission (FCC) rules and regulations; libel, slander and copyright infringement; and the Freedom of Information Act.

Assistant News Director The responsibilities of assistant news directors (sometimes known as managing editors or assignments editors) vary, but often these people are in charge of the day-to-day operation of the newsroom. They assign reporters and news writers to particular news stories and special happenings and may designate technical crews for specific assignments or choose producers for individual newscast segments.

Continuity Writers Contintuity writers are responsible for sales copy for sponsors' products, sometimes for a program, and for handling announcements. These individuals write commercial and promotional copy in support of the station's sales and advertising efforts. Their task is to provide a smooth flow from one segment to the next. At small stations, a salesperson may sometimes fill this role by writing commercials for his or her clients.

Scriptwriters Scriptwriters are in charge of writing scripts for television productions and other programs. This may include documentaries, variety shows, talk shows, situation comedies, and so forth. It also includes assignments offered by companies in many industries, such as manufacturing, government, and education who use videos, generally for viewing by their own employees. For instance, Casual Corner, a large women's clothing concern, uses videos to train its sales staff in the 750 stores across the nation.

Scriptwriting is quite different from other kinds of writing because scriptwriters must think of everything in a visual way so that they can understand how a viewer will experience the program.

Scripts explain both audio and visual elements of productions. The audio section includes the dialogue or narration as well as instructions for sound effects and music. The video portion includes instructions, such as camera angles, and important production information, such as set descriptions and directions to performers.

To develop scripts, writers must focus on the intended audience, the purpose of the program and the subject matter. Then they must do adequate research, organize their findings, and write a script that audiences will understand and enjoy.

Nonfiction programs are sometimes shot before they are written, making the writer fit appropriate words to the visual representation on the screen.

Announcers

Radio and television audiences enjoy getting to know radio and television announcers. Often called disc jockeys since they select and play recorded music, radio announcers sometimes interview guests and present weather, commercials, and sports. If a written script is used, they may also do any research and writing that is necessary, in addition to writing commercial and news copy.

Salary and Employment Outlook

The *Occupational Outlook Handbook* for 1992–1993 compiled by the U.S. Department of Labor reports that salaries in broadcasting vary greatly. Figures for television are higher than radio, large markets bring higher salaries than smaller ones, and commercial broadcasting stations command higher figures than do public broadcasting stations.

According to a survey conducted by the National Association of Broadcasters and the Broadcast Cable Financial Management Association, salaries for experienced radio announcers averaged about $22,000 a year in 1990. Results showed figures of $13,000 in the smallest markets to $54,000 for on-air personalities, $52,000 for sports reporters, and $41,000 for news announcers in the largest markets.

Among television announcers, news anchors averaged $52,000, ranging from $27,000 in the smallest markets to $129,000 in the largest markets. Weatherpeople averaged $43,000, ranging from $25,000 to $98,000. Sportscasters averaged $40,000, ranging from $23,000 to $109,000.

U.S. TELEVISION STATIONS

Atlanta	Chicago
WAGA-TV	WBBM-TV
WATL-TV	WLS-TV
WGNX-TV	WGN-TV
WPBA-TV	WMAQ-TV

Boston	Cleveland
WCVB-TV	WEWS-TV
WGBH-TV	WKYC-TV
WHDH-TV	WOIO-TV
WFXT-TV	WUAB-TV

Dallas–Fort Worth
KDAF-TV
KERA-TV
KTVT-TV
KDFI-TV

Detroit
WDIV-TV
WXON-TV
WTVS-TV
WKBD-TV

Los Angeles
KABC-TV
KTTV-TV
KVEA-TV
KCET-TV

Minneapolis–St. Paul
KARE-TV
KSTP-TV
KTCA-TV
KTMA-TV

Philadelphia
WCAU-TV
WYBE-TV
WGBS-TV
WTXF-TV

Pittsburgh
KDKA-TV
WTAE-TV
WPTT-TV
WQED-TV

St. Louis
KETC-TV
KMOV-TV
KTVI-TV
KDNL-TV

San Francisco–Oakland
KGO-TV
KPIX-TV
KCNS-TV
KRON-TV

Washington, DC
WETA-TV
WRC-TV
WTTG-TV
WUSA-TV

U.S. RADIO STATIONS
Atlanta
WFOX-FM
WGST
WZGC-FM
WCNN

Boston
WBZ
WEEI
WILD
WZLX-FM

Chicago
WBBM-AM/FM
WGN
WIND
WLS

Cleveland
WABQ
WERE
WHK
WJMO

Dallas–Fort Worth
KAAM
KFJZ
KLIF
WBAP

Detroit
WCAR
WCXI
WJR
WJLB

Los Angeles
KABC
KALI
KBRT
KLAC

Minneapolis–St. Paul
KLBB
KMZZ
KYCR
KNOF-FM

Philadelphia
KYW
WHAT
WIP
WZZD

Pittsburgh
KDKA
KQV
WMAO-FM
WBZZ-FM

St. Louis
KASP
KSTL
KUSA
KXEN

San Fransisco-Oakland
KEST
KFAX
KGO
KIQI

Washington, D.C.
WABS
WCTN
WOL
WXTR

CANADIAN TELEVISION STATIONS

Toronto, Ontario
CICA-TV
CITY-TV
CFTO-TV
CFMT-TV

Ottawa, Ontario
CJOH-TV
CBOT-TV

London, Ontario
CFPL-TV

Montreal, Quebec
CFCF-TV
CBMT-TV

Vancouver, British Columbia
KVOS-TV

CANADIAN RADIO STATIONS

Toronto, Ontario
CKEY
CKCC

Qué, Quebec
CBVE-FM

Vancouver, British Columbia
CFUN

Winnipeg, Manitoba
CJOB

London, Ontario
CIXX-FM

Winnipeg, Manitoba
CITI-FM

Windsor, Ontario
CIMX-FM

A CLOSER LOOK AT.......

Sylvia Perez
WLS-TV Channel 7 Anchor

Tell us about your career background.

I attended journalism school at the University of Oklahoma and began my journalism career in 1983. My first job was in my hometown, Lawton, Oklahoma. I did morning news cut-ins and daily reporting. Eventually I was moved to weekend anchor and reporter. In 1984, I went to work for another small station in Amarillo, Texas. Television was just beginning to use live satellite units, and since our station in Lawton did not have live capabilities, I decided to move to one that did. This was an exciting time in my life. I received a phone call from an agent who had seen my tape (demo tape showing a sample of her work) and wanted to know if I would be interested in being represented by that company. They had already sent my tape on to Denver, Colorado, where they showed interest. So after only six months in Amarillo, I moved to Denver, Colorado, as a morning news anchor and weekday reporter. I was still fairly inexperienced, having only worked in a small market. Here I was, headed to a medium-sized market in an exciting city with a very professional newscast.

After two years in Denver, however, the hours were starting to get to me. I had to be in at 4 a.m. to write the news for the 6 a.m. show.

That meant I had to get to bed early to get a decent night's sleep and be up at 2:30 a.m. to get to work. This was very difficult, and since I didn't appear to see any upward movement, I decided to move on.Out of the blue I received a call from an NBC station. The news director said, "I've seen your tape. How would you like to be a weekend anchor in Houston?" He practically tried to hire me on the phone, but I flew out for the interview and decided it would be a good career move. I stayed there for two years as a weekend anchor and medical reporter. However, I decided that medical reporting was not for me. With the help of my agent, I received several job offers, including two in Chicago. I chose WLS-TV where I was hired as a weekend anchor and weekday reporter. Last September (1992) I became the co-anchor of Eyewitness News with Linda Yu at 11:30 a.m., the first newscast in Chicago anchored by two women.

What are your responsibilities?

After I get off the air at noon, I am usually assigned a story unless something breaks, then I get pulled off the story and go cover the late-breaking news. I go out on the street, do the interviews, and write my story which is either presented live or a self-contained piece for one of the newscasts, usually at 5:00 or 6:00 p.m., sometimes 4:00 and 6:00 p.m., depending on how important the story is.

What's a typical work day like for you?

A typical day means *rush, rush, rush.* Since I don't get off the air until noon, I get a late start on my story, a story that someone from another station may be covering and probably started much earlier. That means I have to work fast in order to get everything ready for the newscast. I have to be thorough and make sure I don't miss any important details even though I may only have a short time to put the story together.

What's the best part of working in the field?

A true journalist who loves the job has to be in the field. It's what it's all about, going out and doing the interviews, meeting the people, and having the background and knowledge to put the story together from first-hand experience.

What's the worst part of this job?

The worst part of this job is having to deal with the death and destruction that too many times make up a news story. It's hard to knock on someone's door who has just lost a loved one or is accused of a crime or had some other personal tragedy.

What do you think the station looks for in new candidates?

They look for aggressive reporters who aren't afraid to *work, work, work.* It's a 24-hour job, seven days a week, meaning you always have to be available. You must be eager to learn because you deal with different situations every day, some you may not be familiar with, but you have to be flexible and absorb the information so that you can translate it to viewers. You have to be quick on your feet because too many times you won't have time to prepare a breaking news story. You may have to go live as soon as you arrive on the scene.

What suggestions would you make to others considering this kind of work?

I would say be aware of what you're getting into. It's not the glamorous job everyone thinks. Sitting behind the studio anchor desk is only a small part of the job. It's hard, demanding, and extremely, I repeat extremely, competitive. If you're not committed, you'll never make it. Things have changed and stations no longer want simple news readers. You have to be able to go out on the street; get your hands dirty; and *work, work, work.*

In college, it's advisable to take English, social studies, political science, geography, and journalism classes. As a general assignment reporter, it is most important that you are well rounded.

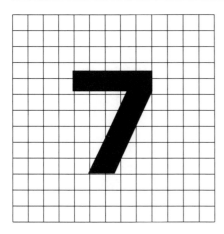

TECHNICAL WRITING

Writing doesn't get easier with experience. The more you know, the harder it is to write.

—Tim O'Brien

Does the following want ad pinpoint an area that is of interest to you? If so, consider the world of the technical writer.

> Technical writer wanted by Fortune 500 company to write wide assortment of technical and product literature. Assignments vary from highly technical data sheets to technical and promotional brochures, and magazine articles in a department that is responsible for the creation of technical publications from concept to printed page. Applicant must have technical aptitude and excellent interpersonal skills to interface with research, engineering, and service departments. Degree in technical writing or related field preferred. Send resume and salary history to Tops Industries, 116 Park Avenue, New York, NY 00001.

If you've tried to put a sound system or bicycle together strictly on the basis of the instructions, you are familiar with one of the responsibilities of a technical writer: to explain scientific and technical concepts in everyday language so the average person can understand them. Companies strive to provide easy-to-understand support literature with their products so buyers may operate equipment as quickly (and painlessly) as possible.

Technical writers must be excellent communicators, translating information into a form that is understandable to the target audience, whether that is the general public or a more specialized group. The Society of Technical Communication explains that "technical communicators serve as the bridge between those who create ideas and those who use them."

Another important job that technical writers perform is writing documentation for computer programs. Products that are touted to be "user friendly" (easy to understand and follow) are expected to have instructions that make this friendliness a reality. Whether they succeed or not is crucial to the sales of computer equipment in the constantly evolving, continually widening, competitively gigantic computer industry.

Technical writers may write about two types of computer products: 1) hardware (the equipment itself, which includes mainframes, the huge computers used by big business) and microcomputers, used by individuals at home or in the office; and 2) software, which refers to the directions that run computer programs (stored on tapes and floppy disks).

Some technical writers compose articles and reports on current trends in the scientific and technological communities. In many cases, they are current or former members of these communities. Other technical writers create press releases and other promotional materials for a variety of clients who wish to sell a product or a service.

Another possibility for technical writers is employment by research laboratories to write reports on research projects, in fields from genetics to space flight. They may also write grant proposals on behalf of research organizations in the hopes of acquiring money for future projects.

Technical writers perform an importance service for the military by writing the training manuals issued to enlistees. These manuals cover details on the operation of equipment and weapons, everything from rifles to computers.

Nonscientific segments of the community may also seek out technical writers. For example, insurance companies hire technical writers to explain terms and procedures to insurance agents, claims adjusters, and others who work in this industry. Other possibilities include writing policies and procedures for any type of operation, from banking to international trading; putting together reports for stockholders; writing booklets or pamphlets on company policies or employee benefits; and preparing reports on the activities of one department in a company to be distributed to the rest of the company.

Technical writers are hired by a multitude of industries including aviation, electronics, chemicals, telecommunications, and pharmaceuticals. As employees of the federal government, they write the many pamphlets published by the U.S. Government Printing Office. These publications cover topics such as education, medicine, aerospace, and agriculture.

Employers include the U.S. Departments of the Interior, Agriculture, Health and Human Services, the National Aeronautics and Space Administration, and the largest federal employer, the Department of Defense.

Technical writers may work for newspaper, magazine, or book publishers; advertising agencies; business or trade publications; professional journals; or colleges and universities. Many work on a freelance basis, meeting the needs of many employers and being paid for each piece they produce.

As an entry-level employee at a company, technical writers begin by assisting experienced writers. This may involve proofreading other writers' work, updating copy, and familiarizing themselves with the style and approach of the company.

Technical writers may also decide to shift their focus from writing to editing. Or, once they acquire more skills, technical writers may move on to becoming project leaders, documentation managers, or specialists in one particular area. Most writers do some editing, of course, but editors carry the bulk of this responsibility. Thus a technical writer can move from creating his or her own text to editing the text of others.

THE DUTIES OF A TECHNICAL WRITER

Initially, the most important factor for a technical writer to determine is *who* is going to read the material. Every document written by a technical writer is intended for a very specific audience, and it is crucial that the proper language is used and appropriate information is included. For instance, mathematical equations would be all right to include for engineers but most likely confusing for the general population.

Once the target audience is established, technical writers discuss the project with program leaders and the scientist or engineer who is designing it; they then begin their exploration for data. After performing extensive research through studying reports, scientific drawings, and scientific and trade journals, they interview engineers, scientists, supervisors, technicians, and anyone else familiar with the topic or procedure they will be writing about. They also carefully study mock-ups, instruments, or equipment, observing any factors or procedures that have a bearing on the project.

Once they have finished their legwork, they organize their notes in a logical sequence, write an outline, and then create a first draft. Technical experts may be called on to scrutinize the document to make sure the technical writer fully understands the concepts involved. Many drafts later, the piece is passed on to an editor or other specialist.

Pictures are often very important in furthering the understanding of those reading technical writers' work. So technical writers must be able to complement the documents they create with visual representations (including tables, charts, diagrams, photos, and illustrations) in order to make the concepts and directions as clear as possible.

A talented technical writer may be likened to a news reporter; a journalist who visits the scene, finds out the details, and prepares the most complete and well-written report as quickly as possible. Of course, a reporter's deadline is likely to be considerably shorter.

The responsibilities of a technical writer may be great, such as in the case of writing up the data on a new medicine. It is possible that a life may depend on his or her correctly discussing side effects, maximum dosages, and contraindications with other medicines.

SKILLS AND REQUIREMENTS FOR TECHNICAL WRITING

Above everything else, a technical writer needs scientific or technical knowledge, a logical mind, and excellent writing skills. A logical mind is necessary because much of a technical writer's work requires putting together pieces of puzzles. Crossword puzzle or cryptogram aficionados have good potential! Inquiring minds will seek out information, determine the relationships between factors, and ascertain how one process is related to or leads to another. Like a doctor faced with a new set of symptoms or a detective faced with a new crime, the technical writer must decipher the subject so the rest of the world can understand it.

Technical writers must also be self-disciplined and organized. They often work alone on projects and must set goals for themselves in order to meet deadlines. In addition, they must be patient enough to work on projects that may extend over many months and flexible enough to work on several projects simultaneously.

Technical writers (and all writers for that matter) must be able to put words together in a clear, concise way to accomplish their purpose. After all, there is a plethora of ways to say the same thing, and writers must ascertain the way that best communicates their idea and purpose. Technical writing, is a craft, not a science. According to Gary Blake and Robert W. Bly in *The Elements of Technical Writing* (Writer's Digest Books, 1993), good technical writing is technically accurate; useful; concise; complete; clear; consistent; correct in spelling, punctuation, and grammar; targeted; well organized; and interesting.

While the subject of the writing is technical and therefore based on fact, all technical writing does not have to contain only dry facts. Some technical writing will also include emotion, such as in composing a company progress report. The writer will present the facts and figures but will also try to make the report look as positive for the company as possible.

Most companies require candidates to have a college degree, most commonly in technical communications, journalism, communications, or English. They may also desire additional courses or experience in a specific or technical area, perhaps engineering or business. Some companies prefer candidates with engineering or science degrees who have some background in journalism. Popular areas include computer science, mathematics, electronics, medicine, agriculture, layout, and design. A knowledge of other languages, such as German, Spanish, Russian, French, and Japanese, may also be considered a plus.

SALARY AND EMPLOYMENT OUTLOOK

The U.S. Department of Labor's *Occupational Outlook Handbook* for 1992–1993 reports that the 1990 Technical Communicator's Salary Survey of median annual salaries revealed the following:

Entry level	$24,000
Mid-level nonmanagement	$34,000
Mid-level management	$38,000
Senior management	$45,000

Technical writers and editors in the federal government averaged $36,897 in 1991, and other writers and editors averaged $35,635.

The demand for technical writers is expected to increase due to the continuing expansion of scientific and technical information and the continued need for communication. The outlook for technical writers is good through the year 2005 because there are a limited number of writers who can handle technical material.

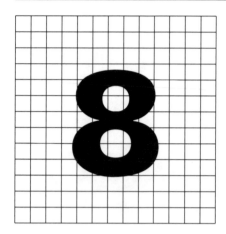

EDUCATION

Acquire new knowledge whilst thinking over the old, and you may become a teacher of others.

—Confucius

While knowledge is one barometer for measuring the effectiveness of a teacher, a number of other qualities are equally important.

If you possess a genuine desire to educate people, are an able communicator, enjoy interacting with others, are highly motivated and organized, and have patience and a sense of humor, then the field of teaching needs you!

Teaching offers many intrinsic rewards but requires a lot of hard work, both physically and mentally. However, you cannot underestimate the feeling you get when you see a "light bulb" go off in a student's head, when a connection is made or a concept is absorbed. It's a feeling without description.

Many decide to teach because they wish to share their love for a particular subject with others. Some feel teaching is a secure profession (at least once tenure is established). And some are attracted to a stimulating, intellectual atmosphere where a concern for others and the future are shared by many.

Is teaching right for you? Ask yourself the following questions:

1. Am I comfortable speaking in front of and being in charge of a group?
2. Am I a patient person?
3. Am I creative and flexible enough to try different approaches to help my students?
4. Am I confident about my expertise in this field?
5. Am I willing to put in long hours (usually) without great financial reward?
6. Do I have strong people skills?
7. Do I have an enduring enthusiasm for this subject?

If you answered yes to all of these questions, consider teaching as a career!

SECONDARY TEACHERS OF JOURNALISM OR ENGLISH

Almost everyone can remember their favorite high school English or journalism teacher. Why is this so? Because if you are lucky, you gained a strong foundation in writing skills and the confidence to express yourself. This was a great gift. After becoming a teacher, you will be in a position to present this life-long treasure to your students.

Individual requirements for high school teachers may vary from state to state, but all must receive their bachelor's degree from a college or university that has a state-approved teacher's curriculum, including classroom experience as a student teacher (usually for six months). To teach journalism classes, you may major in English or journalism and take education classes, or major in education and take English or journalism classes. Following this, most states require applicants to pass a competency test for teacher certification. These examinations test basic skills, subject matter mastery, and teaching ability.

In some states, you may teach with a provisional certificate as soon as you have a college degree. You can attain regular certification by working with an experienced educator for one or two years in combination with taking the necessary education courses. When renewing teaching certificates, additional coursework perhaps even a master's degree, may be required.

Teachers at the high school level may be employed by public or private schools. Private schools may have less stringent requirements, eliminating the necessity to meet state certification specifications.

Often the writing teacher will be in charge of journalism and creative writing classes in addition to teaching English or possibly even social studies or history.

Some secondary schools hire visiting artists, often poets, for an entire academic year. In this case, as individuals who are acknowledged professionals in their field, they do not have to have teaching credentials or even a college degree.

COLLEGE INSTRUCTORS

College instructors fall into four categories: instructors, assistant professors, associate professors, and professors. (Some schools hire entry-level instructors they call lecturers.) Attaining tenure is important to those in this field. New employees are hired and given year-to-year contracts, usually for seven years. The American Association of University Professors (AAUP) recommends that "beginning with appointment to the rank of full-time instructor or a higher rank, the probationary period should not exceed seven years." During the probationary time, individuals are closely scrutinized through a very rigorous screening process, including review by superiors, peers, and the student body, to determine whether they are people the university values enough to keep until retirement. Published work is usually necessary to obtain a tenured position, the quantity depends on the university and what level an educational professional is striving for (full professor, associate professor, and so on). A common phrase among higher education professionals, "Publish or perish," is based in truth. As a result, faculty members at most universities do a considerable amount of research and submission to scholarly journals, those at four-year institutions somewhat less. Professors in the arts may receive credit for published work by writing plays or novels. At two-year (junior) colleges, usually very little research and publication is required, but staff members often teach a greater number of classes.

For the most part, educators teaching at the college level have doctoral degrees. Those teaching at junior colleges often have master's degrees. At four-year universities, associate professors have a minimum of three years of teaching experience at the university level and possess a doctoral degree. Full professors have completed a doctoral program (or a terminal degree if a doctorate is not appropriate), have an excellent established teaching record, and have proven successful in research and teaching. However, quota systems at some schools may limit the number of individuals who can take on a higher rank.

At junior colleges, educators are usually given two or three years before an evaluation is conducted and those who are deemed worthy are granted tenure.

There is considerable variance in how departments and classes are arranged. For instance, creative writing, composition, and technical writing may be offered through the English department (and those who teach these classes may also teach literature classes). Communications and journalism may even be divided into separate departments. Within these departments will be public relations writing and advertising. Some smaller schools offer only a handful of courses, and they may be placed in the theater, English, speech, or other department.

Instructors may teach advertising, journalism, film, and television classes and may hold any rank from instructor to full professor at the undergraduate or graduate level. More specifically, there are classes in news writing, news gathering, radio, video, news management, the history of broadcasting, television production, and filmmaking.

Classes range from huge lecture halls filled with many students to small groups (particularly at the graduate level) where considerable individual attention may be given. In this case, sessions are seminars where there is likely to be a more personal give-and-take atmosphere. Sometimes teaching assistants lead group discussions after lectures, and the instructor or professor may supervise and observe his or her teaching assistant.

The customary teaching load ranges from 12 to 16 hours each week, not counting preparation time and staff meetings or conferences. Students are usually required to prepare written assignments, term papers, and other reports; thus, the instructor must read, evaluate, and grade each student's work. Additionally, teachers have a number of other responsibilities. They are expected to advise students about courses, career direction, or any other matter of concern. This adds another three to six hours per week, often in the form of standard office hours when students know teachers are available to them. Staff members may also be expected to assist with registration, special projects, internships, and graduate theses, in addition to serving on department and university committees and developing proposals for research grants and administering them. Department heads have additional responsibilities.

Some community and adult education schools offer writing courses in addition to those available through correspondence schools. For the most part, these programs do not lead to a degree.

Writers who teach and teachers who write generally agree that the teaching keeps them alert and proficient as writers. Often, instructors begin teaching after they have had some measure of success as authors, journalists, freelance writers, television or radio personalities, or other media professionals. By teaching others to write, they are indeed stronger, more proficient writers themselves.

SALARY AND EMPLOYMENT OUTLOOK

The *Occupational Outlook Handbook* for 1992–1993 reports that, according to the National Education Association, public secondary school teachers averaged about $33,700 a year in 1990–1991. Earnings in private schools were generally lower.

Employment of secondary school teachers is expected to rise to greater than average for all occupations through 2005 as high school enrollments grow and class sizes diminish. Another factor is the large number of teachers who will reach retirement age then.

According to a 1990–1991 survey by the American Association of University Professors, the average salary for full-time faculty members was $43,700. The average for professors was $56,200; associate professors, $41,800; assistant professors, $34,600; and instructors, $26,100.

College instructors are often given sabbatical leave (one year every seven years) for which they receive a half year's salary. They often have excellent benefits, including group life insurance, free tuition at the college, retirement plans, free access to athletic and social events, and fellowships at home or abroad.

A CLOSER LOOK AT.......

Charles-Gene McDaniel
Head, Faculty of Journalism and Communication Studies, Roosevelt University, Chicago, Illinois

Describe your educational background.

As an undergraduate, I attended Northwestern University's Medill School of Journalism where I minored in psychology, received the Shuman Award in English Composition, and earned a Bachelor of Science degree. Continuing further, I received my Master of Science degree in Journalism, also from Medill. One summer I enjoyed a special International Summer School study program in Cambridge, England. The focus was British literature.

Where did your career go from there?

I worked as a reporter at *The Gazette and Daily* in York, Pennsylvania (now called the York *Daily Record*). I then spent many years as a writer, science writer, and editor for the Associated Press, Chicago Bureau. My special interest is in the behavioral sciences. When I made the switch to academia, I came to Roosevelt as an Associate Professor of English and Communicative Arts and director of the Journalism Program.

What is a typical day like?

A typical day is *frantic*—possibly twelve hours with no lunch break! To put it mildly, academia is a challenge. I thought being a full-time journalist was hectic, but this beats that. And our work doesn't end when we leave the university for the day. We have papers to grade every week from every class, especially in this field. That takes care of nights and weekends. I don't think people appreciate how many hours we put in. And some of us do research in addition. I get great joy out of teaching, but unfortunately we have a lot more to do than teach. There are many extra jobs which take us away from teaching; extra chores like recruiting, which we do gladly because we believe in the students and the school. But it does make our schedules very pressured.

When I came here there were 40 students and we now have more than 600. We still devote as much time as we possibly can individually so that our students do not feel that they are just a social security number. Thus, we get to know our students and their strengths. The personal contact, though taxing on the faculty, has shown to produce successful results for some of the students who have graduated from the program.

How did you decide to go into teaching?

Journalism and teaching are much alike, both didactic. In journalism, we go out and learn all we can and then we write about it so we can teach our readers or our viewers. In education, we learn and then we teach our students what we have learned. For me, it was a natural transition from full-time journalist to full-time teacher, part-time journalist. As a journalist, I am the Chicago correspondent for a medical post in Toronto and for Encyclopedia Britannica where I write articles for the *Medical and Health Yearbook*.

In the initial class session of each introductory journalism course, I always quote from Chaucer from the *Student's Tale:* "And gladly would he learn, And gladly teach." Those are my feelings exactly!

What's the best part of your position?

The best part is the teaching, working with the students and taking pride in their achievements. Some of them do well after they leave here.

What would you say about the possibilities of entering the world of journalism?

I would say that journalism is a wide field with many opportunities in various areas. There's much more than newspapers and magazines. For instance, Chicago is the world center for trade journal publishing. In fact, Frank Baum was working for a Chicago trade journal when he wrote *The Wizard of Oz.* You have your choice of newsletters, specialty magazines, television stations, cable companies, to name only a few. There are many possibilities. And don't ever dismiss the rewards of working on a small publication where you can discern very direct results. On a national media level, you're not in touch with the people who read your work and are influenced by it, so it's difficult to tell whether you're having any effect or not. Not so for small publications where you can effect change in a community.

What advice would you give those considering this field?

You must have the ability to write and have command of the English language. Even though we shouldn't be teaching the basics at this level, often we have to because reporting is basic. You have to be able to convey your ideas in such a way that people can understand them. If you don't have basic grammar, spelling, and punctuation skills, you won't be understood. In journalism, the product has always been important because it doesn't make any difference what the process is if you can't decipher the product.

I would advise that you write a simple resume presenting evidence that shows you are qualified for the job. Offer clips and other evidence of commitment. Create a network of people and contacts. Go to meetings where you'll meet journalists and others in publishing. Make yourself known; be assertive in presenting yourself, don't hold back.

Polish your aggressive personality. The press serves as the watchdog of democracy so it is up to us as journalists to serve as a surrogate of society in questioning authority.

Professor Charles-Gene McDaniel is the recipient of many awards: two from the Illinois State Medical Society for medical journalism, two from the

Chicago Institute for Psychoanalysis for interpreting psychoanalysis to the
public, and the American Psychological Association's Distinguished Contributor Award for magazine writing (1982). He is listed in *Who's Who in
American Education, 1990–, Who's Who in U.S. Writers, Editors & Poets,
1988–,* and *Who's Who in America, 1975–.* McDaniel's work has appeared in
dozens of magazines, periodicals, and other publications. He makes guest
appearances as a speaker, lecturer, and panelist at medical and journalism
schools, civic groups, scientific and health conferences, and other groups, in
addition to radio and television appearances.

BUSINESS WRITING

Blot out, correct, insert, refine, Enlarge, diminish, interline;
Be mindful, when invention fails, To scratch your head, and
bite your nails.

—Jonathan Swift

The following challenges were offered publicly in the *New York Times* on November 30, 1984, by J. Walter Thompson, one of the largest advertising agencies in the world. The headline read "Write If You Want Work." How well would you do?

1. In 100 words tell how you would sell a telephone to a Trappist monk who is under a strict vow of silence.
2. Make a can of baked beans sound mouthwatering.
3. Compose a speech welcoming a delegation of Martians to Central Park using only pictures and symbols.

ADVERTISING COPYWRITERS

Copywriters are creative souls who work with ideas, images, details, words, and concepts to produce scintillating, fresh copy for their clients. They are the ones who compose the ads, including headlines and "body copy" of enticing word assemblage, that we find in magazines, on billboards, and on the lips of actors and television announcers. Those who attain success are clever, talented, quick-witted, strong writers who are knowledgeable about their product and the world in general.

The copywriter is part of a creative team consisting of one or more creative directors or copywriters, art directors, and producers. Work is approached as a team effort and individuals collaborate to produce the best possible campaign. No definitive lines are drawn; copywriters may come up with visual ideas and art directors may devise the headline.

For television commercials, copywriters and art directors do more than write copy and present visuals; they must present a theme, format, music, and special effects. A storyboard is used to show the script for the television commercial along with drawings of what will appear on screen.

All jobs begin with a thorough understanding of the client's needs, desires, and goals, as well as the audience being targeted. Then the research begins. Copywriters and assistants dig, dig, dig to find out everything that would help them convey the client's product or service in the best possible way. This may mean that the creative team meets with experts in related fields, such as medicine, psychology, law, social sciences, and education. Interviews are conducted with those close to the situation, libraries are scoured, and other resources are tapped.

Once the creative team is satisfied with their genius, they present their ideas to their clients, hoping they will be receptive. Thus, copywriters need to be capable, persuasive speakers, able to win clients over.

Robert W. Bly's *The Copywriter's Handbook,* (Henry Holt and Company, 1985) provides a checklist for copywriters that reveals excellent insights into the difficult job they perform:

Does the copy fulfill the promise of the headline?

Is the copy interesting?

Is it easy to read?

Is it believable?

Is it persuasive?

Is it specific?

Is it concise?

Is it relevant?

Does it flow smoothly?

Does it call for action?

Copywriters are employed by advertising agencies, but they also work for many corporations that have communications or marketing departments where copywriting is a priority. Other possibilities are newspapers and magazines that have employees who help advertisers with their ads, book publishers that maintain advertising personnel, and self-employment as a freelance copywriter.

Copywriters may also write and edit public service copy for any number of social issues, such as rape victims, the handicapped, and the homeless. To execute this intelligently, writers must encourage rather than frighten and emphasize the possibilities for adjustment or cure. Some copywriters specialize in a particular area, such as fashion, computers, electronics, medicine, or finance.

Individuals often enter this field as junior copywriters or even as secretaries or copy assistants. Though performing less desirable work at this level, they learn the fundamentals of the business. At the other end of the hierarchy at larger agencies, there may be copy supervisors, copy chiefs, or copy directors who make assignments and supervise the employees and their copy.

The *Occupational Outlook Handbook* for 1992–1993 indicates that a growth of advertising and public relations agencies should be a source of new jobs through the year 2005.

QUESTION: What do Theodore Dreiser, Cornelia Otis Skinner, Sinclair Lewis, and Bob Newhart have in common?

ANSWER: They all worked in advertising as copywriters!

PUBLIC RELATIONS SPECIALISTS

Public relations is hardly a new concept. Its practice dates back to 1787 when the Constitutional Convention employed people to encourage others to ratify the Constitution. Both North and South used the media to present and persuade others to share their views during the Civil War.

The goal then was as it is now—to build, maintain, and promote beneficial relationships between two factions or in today's world, for the most part, between companies and the public they serve. Public relations writing aims to build a positive image, present an enterprise in a favorable light, or advocate a position.

Public relations specialists work for all kinds of organizations: hospitals, colleges and universities, political parties, government agencies, social welfare groups, nonprofit organizations, and many other kinds of companies and associations. Individuals may work for companies that have public relations staff or public relations firms hired by companies that seek their services.

Business and industry use public relations to educate the masses about the availability of their products or services. This is called *corporate public relations*. Schools, hospitals, churches, and social welfare groups use public relations as a public service. This is called *public information* or *nonprofit public relations*. Since nonprofit organizations do not advertise, this is the only way to get the word out.

Public relations specialists may conduct market research (surveys) to determine how the public feels about a company and its products or services. They then analyze their findings, write formal reports, and set up programs to promote these ideas or products by working with the media of television, cable television, radio, newspapers, magazines, and other printed forms of communication.

Generally, there are six basic categories of public relations work.

1. *Research.* This is the preliminary work that must always be done to define the client's goals and decide the best way to achieve them. Interviews, surveys, library research, opinion polls, and data collection are all part of this stage.
2. *Program work.* After the research is done, the findings are analyzed, and a strategy is planned.

3. *Writing and editing.* This includes internal memos and reports, written presentations to clients, letters to solicit endorsements, and press releases. There may also be shareholder reports, film scripts, and magazine articles.

4. *Special events.* These may be anything from press conferences to guest appearances to rock concerts. All must be carefully planned to gain considerable public attention.

5. *Media placement.* This involves selecting the material to be released, who to release it to, and the timing of the release.

6. *Fundraising.* This is an important endeavor for nonprofit organizations. Activities include benefit dinners, membership appeals, direct-mail solicitation, and radio and television fund drives.

Top managers or directors of public relations firms review campaigns and budgets, supervise all personnel, and strive to develop new clients. Middle positions may be filled by account executives. Entry-level office assistants answer phones, maintain files, search through and clip out newspaper and magazine articles, perform research, write media releases and short articles, formulate media lists, and aid in special events.

OTHER FORMS OF BUSINESS WRITING

Business communicators include writers and editors, photographers and artists, audiovisual experts, and graphic designers. Writing for business may take many forms, from the speech written for the business executive, to the corporation's yearly report, to a company newsletter. Any type of company, from a local dog kennel to a chic boutique, may seek out and benefit from the services of business-writing specialists.

Writing or editing for companies may be done for both internal and external communications. External communications include business letters, promotional letters, press releases, brochures, catalogs, news stories, flyers, and instructional manuals. Internal communications may include employees' newsletters, magazines, annual and quarterly reports, program evaluations, handbooks, instruction manuals, and policy manuals. Writers are given the responsibility for generating article ideas, interviewing related parties, performing necessary research, and organizing and writing the business communications. In addition to copy, writers may be responsible for selecting artwork, charts, and any other visual aids.

Business firms and nonprofit groups, such as the Juvenile Diabetes Association, the American Red Cross, and the United Fund, in addition to other community social agencies, major cultural institutions and fund drives, both large and small, hire business writers for their consumer publications, catalogs, and handbooks. These publications are designed to bring the organizations' causes to the public's attention and to enhance public good will.

Additionally, most utility companies and investment houses, banks, health care organizations, hospitals, art museums, and zoos, regularly send out newsletters or magazines. Using flyers, bulletins, letters, and brochures, they strive to raise funds, publicize their organization, and encourage people to participate in their special events. A tremendous amount of research, creativity, and writing ability goes into these efforts. Some may be done by advertising copywriters, but much is not.

There are many newsletters written by professional business journalists, including the following: *Daily Labor Report,* which covers labor law and legislation affecting a number of industries; *Hospital Risk Management,* which covers the prevention of liability in hospitals; *Tax-Exempt News,* which features developments that affect charities and other tax-exempt groups; *Federal Budget Report,* which covers the President's budget and the congressional appropriations process; *Oil Express,* which covers petroleum marketing; and *Drug Enforcement Report,* which covers federal antidrug policies and programs.

There is another important function business writers may provide—writing seminars or courses geared to new employees or to update long-time employees. Many companies feel they are receiving an excellent return on their money when they increase the proficiency of their staff's writing abilities. These classes might address problems such as helping draft standard letters in their most efficient, persuasive way or formulating company stock reports so stockholders can more easily comprehend the data. Writing basics (spelling, punctuation, and grammar) are covered, in addition to tips for writing clearer correspondence and keeping the target audience in mind. Business areas that could benefit from these services include research and development, medical writing, library science, financial analysis, manufacturing, marketing, production, and personnel and training. For personnel, language used in job descriptions and the writing and interpreting of personnel evaluations for large firms is very important. There may also be manuals and training guides, tests, application forms, and questionnaires for this department.

A CLOSER LOOK AT.......

Christen P. Heide
Executive Editor for Sales and Marketing Publications, The Dartnell Corporation

Tell us about your educational background.

I attended Lawrence University (Appleton, Wisconsin), the University of Pittsburgh (Pittsburgh, Pennsylvania), and the University of Wisconsin in

Madison, Wisconsin, concentrating in philosophy and English and earning a double major. The two fields are an excellent combination; philosophy gives you the "big picture" and teaches you how to think by giving you a good grounding in logic. English, literature, creative writing, and basic grammar give you the tools to put your thoughts on paper.

Interestingly, back in the late '60s and early '70s, some employers viewed a journalism degree as a negative. In fact, the editorial department of one 80,000 circulation daily paper made a point of not hiring journalism graduates. You were hired on the basis of interest in the field and writing ability. (And if you had an insatiable desire to work terrible hours for low pay, the hiring decision was easier still). In the beginning, you go where the work is; later you can be selective. For me, this meant positions at Reader's Digest in New York City, Ad/Mar Research in New York City, a variety of freelance jobs in New York; the *Milwaukee Star News,* a Milwaukee weekly; *The News-Gazette* and the *Journal Herald* in Winchester, Indiana; and the *Journal Gazette* in Fort Wayne, Indiana. The positions ranged from reporter to managing editor.

Tell us about your responsibilities at Dartnell.

My main responsibility is to direct the editorial focus and content of the sales and marketing publications from conceptualization to final printed product. I function as editor and/or author for other printed material on an as-needed basis.

My general editorial duties focus on generating appropriate articles for publication. This includes assigning articles to freelance writers, working with outside public relations firms, research companies, CEOs, presidents, sales managers, and the like to develop story ideas and produce finished stories.

I edit, rewrite, or self-generate all materials for publication. This includes specifying type, writing headlines, selecting photos and/or graphics, writing captions, and general layout.

Functioning as survey director and author for our Sales Force Compensation Survey, I work closely with Sales and Marketing Executives International headquarters to produce an association newsletter.

I am also responsible for training new editors and working with department heads on an as-needed, per-project basis.

Other duties include providing media interviews as necessary and maintaining ongoing press relations and author contacts.

What is a typical day like?

All days are similar in one respect; they are focused around producing publications on schedule. Activities that take you away from this are very much a part of the job and must be dealt with creatively. Deadline pressure is a constant; however, you have a great deal of freedom determining how to spend your time. The one catch is, when the time is up, you'd better be ready! Playing catch up is nerve-racking and detracts from quality. *So* many things must get done at the same time.

What's the best part of working in this field?

There is a wonderful sense of accomplishment when major projects are completed. Working in a creative field brings great satisfaction; something brand new exists because of your efforts.

Unlike other occupations, journalists can continue to work on a freelance basis after normal retirement. Carpenters, for instance, face the limitations of age and physical ability. But writing requires very little of a person physically. As long as you can think and hold a pencil, you can work almost anywhere. This type of career can give you untold amounts of freedom.

What's the worst part of the job?

Any job can get tedious if you let it. But if you keep challenging yourself, the monotonous parts will be easier to take.

What would you recommend to others considering entering this field?

Anyone considering this field must like to read, like to be challenged, and like hard work. I would recommend that you learn all you can about word usage, grammar, etc. and really know it well. Many people wash out because they don't have the basic foundation of skills. You've got to be detail minded and take pride in a job well done. Mistakes are costly.

What someone really needs is a love of language in order to appreciate its nuances, its richness, its variety, its playfulness. For the power of language lies in its ability to create new thoughts, inspire people to action, amuse and entertain, and pursue the truth.

Christen P. Heide is a respected speaker and writer on the topics of sales compensation and sales force management. His articles have appeared in such publications as *Advertising Age* and *Marketing News,* and he is widely quoted in the business press as a sales and marketing authority. He recently addressed the 54th International Marketing Congress of Sales and Marketing Executives International (SMEI) on contemporary issues in compensation and has been a featured sales compensation speaker at the Sales and Marketing Executives Society of Houston and Sales and Marketing Executives of Corpus Christi, Texas. Additionally, he appeared on *INC.* magazine's

"Fourth Annual Growing The Company Conference" program, where he spoke on using sales incentives to boost sales performance.

A CLOSER LOOK AT.......

Thomas J. Sprtel
Director of Communications and Marketing, Northbrook Park District, Northbrook, Illinois

How did you get started in this field?

As a young child, I always had an interest in the world of broadcasting. I would listen to the Green Hornet, the Misterbrau Showcase, and, as the late fifties arrived, disc jockeys and rock and roll.

Sometime in my early teen years, I met a disc jockey, and he allowed me to visit him at the local station. My awe and excitement only made me want to get more and more involved. Soon I started spinning records for parties and at neighborhood sock hops. By high school, I was doing master of ceremonies work for local high school dances and earning good spending money.

My big day came with the advent of FM radio and a new station to Milwaukee. I was given a chance to host a one-hour show for teens where I could play any records in good taste. This led to another job on a rural radio station north of Milwaukee and a regular show for five hours on Saturday and Sunday.

How did your career progress from there?

After two years of attending the University of Wisconsin in Milwaukee and working part time at the student radio station, I entered the United States Navy in 1966. With my basic training and the advent of the Vietnam War, I was able to become a broadcast journalist for the navy. I hosted daily radio shows to the fleet of ships off Vietnam and had associated duties as a photojournalist and a journalist writing basic media releases about the 7th fleet and their duties during the war. I excelled in photojournalism, having an eye for a good picture: two of which have become part of history. The first, a photo of the HMS Perth being hit by Vietnamese long-range guns in the Tonkin Gulf, was distributed all through the military and in Australian newspapers, and the other, a photo of our captain talking to the men on the ship I was on, (I'm told) hangs in the Pentagon.

The navy was a great place for me. I learned how to expand on my broadcasting experience and added photojournalism and basic journalism to my background. I took specialized training in both areas and spent countless hours with professional photographers. In 1968, I returned to civilian life and entered college again to get at least a two-year degree. Television became my new goal, building on my photography background and my past in radio.

In college, I studied all areas of speech, journalism, and television broadcasting/production and received an Associate Degree in Television Production and graduated tops in my class, with no prospect for a job. I really had no interest to continue for a four-year degree, thinking I could master the world with my applied experiences of the navy, my past radio background, and with TV know-it-all.

I found out the world was not as accommodating as I wished but did locate work in radio where I wound up at Wisconsin's most powerful station in Milwaukee three years later. There I was behind the scenes—first, a music director, picking the records and passing judgment on what music the public wanted. With my efforts and hard work on the part of all station members, the station became number one for five years running and I entered a new area, promotions and publicity.

Countless hours were spent coming up with contest ideas and promotions for the station during its two rating periods each year. A few major promotions made national attention in the radio world. One involved sending two disc jockeys around the world on a "road-rally" style treasure hunt. One DJ went in a westerly direction and the other in an easterly direction. The goal was to follow all instructions given them and see who would return back to Milwaukee first. I had worked on the idea for seven months with American Express and United Airlines. Each DJ received a sealed envelope with instructions to follow. In Milwaukee, their first instructions were to get aboard a certain flight and go to the central American Express office upon arrival. I believe the first stop for the east DJ was London. There, after visiting the central American Express office, he was told to visit Big Ben and have his photo taken by a person to prove he was there, go to Hyde Park and have his photo taken with a soap-box preacher, and then get aboard flight number [such and such], and so on around the world. I remember one DJ was arrested in Turkey for being out after the curfew there, and I was called by the station general manager at 2 a.m. to talk with the State Department. We finally got him released about 5 a.m. and put aboard his next flight. Ah, those fun days of radio and promotions/marketing!

I left radio when I was doing well, thinking I could do better salary-wise elsewhere. Cable TV was coming, and it appealed to me.

I took a job with a national company called SelecTV, which was setting up pay television in Milwaukee. Here, I used my television production background and my skills in promotions/marketing to help drum up publicity for the company. Although the company did well for two years, the breakeven point was so far out due to the high cost of investment that they decided to close after five years. It gave me great experiences though; I was involved with production on pay-per-view national sports baseball games from Milwaukee and Hollywood movies, which required me to make countless visits to Los Angeles and the movie studios. Though I turned down two offers to go west due to the uncertainty of a move to that area, the friends I made were good ones.

After a few positions in nonrelated journalism and promotions, I found myself working for the United States Army at Fort Sheridan as a journalist and media specialist. Somehow I happened to be at the right place at the right time; desktop publishing was the newest innovation. As a civilian, I did media releases for Chicago-area recruiting. With my photo, printing, and journalism background, I was trained on computers and had a natural feel for graphic layout. I enjoyed the work, including taking many of the needed photos I would release to the media.

From there, I joined the Northbrook Park District where my duties include publicity, marketing, and desktop publishing.

What's a typical day like?

There's never a dull day. The park district serves a community of about 30,000 people where recreation and educational programs for preschoolers to seniors are provided year-round. We have one of the best figure-skating programs in the country, a theater which features children's and adult productions, and a very active sports program with everything from basketball to Lacrosse. All in all, I publish three major recreation guides yearly, each at least 48 pages in size.

About 75 percent of my time is involved in desktop publishing and design of the latest recreation magazine. Included in the normal work week are publicity media releases for the programs, photos of activities, and coordination of everything to the public. Other time is spent on program promotional flyers, writing special public service announcements for radio and television, and designing special flyers that are included in local papers as enrollment boosters.

Since I've been involved in Communications and Marketing (formerly called Promotions) and specializing in desktop design, I've won two awards for layout/design of two magazines and their contents. When things get down or the deadlines are fast approaching, I look at these awards and say I did a good job and I can do it again. I like what I do and really wouldn't trade it for any other profession.

Thomas J. Sprtel received awards for the "Best Single Brochure" (layout/design) in the 11th Annual Illinois Parks and Recreation Association (1993); "Best Brochure Cover Photo" in the 11th Annual Illinois Parks and Recreation Association (1993); and the "Best Single Brochure" (layout/design) in the 10th Annual Illinois Parks and Recreation Association (1992).

A CLOSER LOOK AT.......

Noreen Lekas and Joanne Levine
Co-owners, Lekas and Levine Public Relations, Inc., Glenview, Illinois

Tell us about your company.

Lekas and Levine Public Relations, Inc., was established in 1986. We are a small agency whose clients range from small to mid-sized businesses. Since most public relations agencies tend to solicit business among larger companies, ours is somewhat of a special niche in the field. Our staff consists of two equal partners, and we employ a third, part-time assistant during our busiest seasons. During any given month, we service approximately 8 to 12 clients, some of them short-term (perhaps a few months) and others ongoing.

Our company specializes in pursuing media publicity, an aspect of public relations that is probably the most popular among clients. While we do write copy for brochures, business letters, and newsletters; plan minor events; and dabble in a variety of customer requests, 80 percent of our time is spent trying to help our clients make the news. Not to be confused with paid advertising, we are talking about pursuing *editorial* coverage—inclusion in newspaper or magazine articles, radio interviews, television news appearances, and the like. Our clients recognize media publicity as a valuable tool to increase visibility of their products or services, while enhancing their images in the eyes of potential customers, suppliers, competitors, and others. While paid advertising "looks like an ad," editorial appearances add credibility and help to establish our clients as authorities in their respective fields. Whether fledgling entrepreneurs or established pillars of the business community, there are few business owners who wouldn't relish the chance to make a favorable impression in the news.

On the other hand, our specialty is probably the least favorite among public relations practitioners. With an ad, you know what day it will appear, what size it will be, and exactly what it will say. Clients pay by the column inch and are secure in knowing what they are getting for their money. With an article, we all hold our breath until we read it in the paper or magazine. With a taped interview on radio or television, we wait to see whether anything was cut, taken out of context, etc. While our press releases and phone conversations with the editor or writer have been chock full of the kind of information we hope they will relay to the public, there are no guarantees such as those in advertising. Will they interpret our angle the way in which it was intended? Will they mention any competitors? Will the client be quoted accurately and intelligently? Will they remember to give the phone number? Will the whole article be cut at the last minute because of some late-breaking news that requires a large chunk of space in the paper? We work with editors and writers who are always on deadline, always overworked, but nevertheless, always looking for a good angle. For these reasons, ours is a stressful area, often plagued with problems that are completely out of our control.

But when all goes well, there's nothing like it. We have seen the positive results of good, steady media campaigns time and again. And more than once in a while, a "really big" media appearance can make an overnight difference in someone's business. The client is on cloud nine, his or her phones start to ring off the hook with new business, and we are showered with praise and gratitude! It seems that we are often originally hired to promote one particular event, but once the clients get a taste of the benefits of the limelight, we are often asked to continue to work indefinitely. For this reason, we often get to know our clients well and enjoy friendly, upbeat working relationships with them. The knowledge that we are helping to make our clients' businesses grow is very rewarding.

Tell us about your clients.

Over the years, our clients have been as varied as one could possibly imagine. Products we've been associated with include a Missouri farmer's homegrown popcorn, steel-belted radials, palatial greenhouses, yogurt, a $200 summer wardrobe, Federal period antiques, an 88-gallon teak whirlpool bathtub, muscle cars of the '60s, pizza sausage, classical music, and a toilet seat that rotates a thin plastic covering around the seat with the push of a button (no kidding).

Our clients who provide services have been equally diverse: a reggae singer, a foreign marketing consultant, a massage therapy center, a medical illustration firm, a career counseling center, a fashion coordinator and wearable art broker, and a team-based management consultant, to name just a few. Some of our most rewarding experiences have come from helping to promote the services of a financial planning firm specializing in aiding families with severely handicapped dependents and a Chicago-area sheltered workshop and job training program for mentally handicapped adults.

But our favorite client by far has been a small chain of comic bookshops. One of our very first clients, our work with this company has grown for seven years, and we now handle quite a wide variety of their publicity needs. From Spiderman's wedding to Superman's death, we have tied our client into the news surrounding many events that have been in the limelight in this ever-increasingly popular form of entertainment. We've tackled the subjects of the promotion of literacy through comic books, the profitable hobby of collecting comics as an investment, the growth of the industry in general, and the growth of our client's business in particular, from a few small, out-of-the way shops to a group of tantalizing, popular culture emporiums located in upscale malls. The highlight of our duties is the promotion of personal appearances scheduled in the store by popular comic artists and writers, both from the mainstream and from the lesser-known world of alternative comic books.

Describe a typical day.

A typical day at our company begins with what we affectionately refer to as "shuffling," going through each client's file to determine what needs to be done, what calls need to be made, and what submissions need follow-up. It is during this time that we normally make phone calls on their behalf and send out additional press releases or materials (such as photos) that may have been requested by a writer who is working on a story that includes our client. Most important, a lot of strategizing goes on while we shuffle.

We meet with our clients perhaps once a month, some more and some less, as need dictates. These meetings are almost always held at their places of business, so that we get the opportunity to look around, see what's new, and pick up the current buzz. The purpose of these meetings may be to discuss progress, brainstorm new ideas, plan a new project, or conduct an interview in preparation to write a new press release. It's always the most enjoyable part of our day, because we appreciate every opportunity to know our clients a little better and feel a little more involved in their businesses. So much of what we do can be handled by mail, fax, and phone, that we also always appreciate every opportunity to go outside!

Another obviously very important part of our day is writing. Whether it's a letter, news press release, feature article pitch (in the form of a lengthy, more fully developed press release), copy for a brochure, or an article which we are ghostwriting, we choose every single word with a great deal of care. The success or failure of an entire project rests on the written submission, which is always the editor's or writer's first introduction to what we are pitching. Unlike the common misconception that public relations counselors' success depend upon "who they know," our success depends upon presenting good material to the appropriate person in the appropriate manner. Which brings us to one more activity that needs constant attention.

Familiarizing oneself with the media is a never-ending responsibility. We study the papers, magazines, radio, and television programs to which we submit our work, in order to learn what they are looking for. While there are a few good media guides that provide names, this is not a substitute for studying the *style* of an individual person, section, or publication we plan to approach. Also, as the media faces the same recession as the rest of the country, cutbacks and consolidations cause frequent changes in personnel that happen at a pace with which no directory could keep up.

As we look back over the weeks, months, and years, we both agree that the most rewarding part of our effort is the knowledge that we have truly made a difference in our clients' businesses and, consequently, in their lives. The wide diversity of our clientele makes for a job that never gets boring. As we look ahead, more than anything else, we wonder what our next subject will be.

SALARY AND EMPLOYMENT OUTLOOK

According to the *Occupational Outlook Handbook* for 1992–1993, the median earnings for public relations specialists were about $30,000 per year in 1990. Individuals with a bachelor's degree who were employed by the federal government started at $21,000 per year in 1991 and hirees with master's degrees began at $25,700 a year. A report from the College Placement Council reveals that graduates with a bachelor's degree majoring in public relations received starting offers of $20,912 a year (September 1991). Another report from the College and University Personnel Association listed the earnings of chief public relations officers in colleges and universities as $42,298 per year.

According to Carol Kleiman's, *The 100 Best Jobs for the 1990s and Beyond,* public relations specialists soon may need accreditation by the Public Relations Society of America. This requires individuals to have five years' experience in the field and to achieve passing grades on oral and written tests. The book also projects that communications is a growth industry, and by the year 2000, 14,000 additional jobs will be created for public relations specialists. The majority of the demand will spring from the business community, which will want intelligent professionals with experience to present a corporation's best face to the public. However, the *Occupational Outlook Handbook* for 1992–1993 reports that competition for jobs will be keen through the year 2005, particularly among recent college graduates with communications degrees. Those without the appropriate education or experience will face the toughest obstacles in acquiring these jobs.

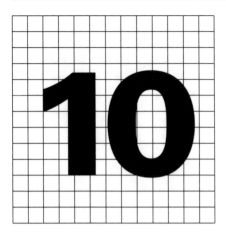

OTHER JOURNALISTIC CAREERS

You're a writer. And that's something better than being a millionaire. Because it's something holy.

—Harlan Ellison

Ellison's words echo the sentiments of many who enter the world of journalism, a world where words provide an avenue for expression, fulfillment, and joy.

FREELANCE WRITERS

Many who share this love become freelance writers, self-employed individuals who work on their own projects and take assignments from employers as they choose. The phrase comes from the Middle Ages and refers to mercenary soldiers or military adventurers, often of knightly rank, who offered their services to any state, party, or cause. So, too, freelance writers offer their services to those who need them. Some freelancers specialize in one area, such as educational writing, and others prefer to perform a variety of writing from novels to feature articles to public relations work.

There are many advantages to operating as a freelancer: You are able to set your own hours; you may work at home (or anywhere else for that matter); you need not purchase a new work wardrobe (anything goes); you are your own boss; you can set up your day-to-day work area any way you wish; you may pick and choose the clients you wish to work with; you have a greater variety of projects to choose from; and you have the freedom to take on as many or as few projects as you wish. On the negative side is the fact that cash flow may be erratic (or nonexistent at times); sometimes you are not even promised payment until something is published (possibly a considerable time after you've written it, even a year or more); the amount of work may be scarce at times; clients don't always pay when they should; you may feel quite isolated; and you don't get the stimulation that you do in working with a staff of other creative beings. Clearly there are many advantages and disadvantages.

One thing is certain though: You shouldn't think of doing this on a full-time basis until a clientele has been built up or you have laid the groundwork for this goal to become a reality. How does a potential freelance writer get to the point where he or she can realistically consider doing this on a full-time basis? This is a difficult question to answer; however, several things need to be taken into consideration. How much money do you need to live on? How many clients can you count on (you never know this for sure, but at least as far as you can tell now)? How much work will you be getting from these clients? How much money does this amount to? Where there is any doubt, the old adage about keeping your day job applies here.

The stories of overnight success are just that—stories. A lot of hard work and perseverance are necessary for any success as a freelance writer (or any kind of journalist for that matter).

Where do you begin? There is no one path that anyone can design for you. Depending on your interests and background, there are many ways to begin in this field.

One common way freelancers start is by writing in an area in which they are familiar. This could be their career, but it could also be a hobby or subject about which they are knowledgeable. Take, for instance, the case of Michael, who has been fascinated with dinosaurs since he was a little boy. Writing about a tyrannosaurus rex would be easy and enjoyable for him. All he would need to do is identify markets that would be interested in his work. A quick trip to the library to search through *Writer's Market, The Writer's Handbook,* or *Literary Market Place* would easily take care of that. (There are many other sources too, but these are three of the most complete and reader friendly). In order to clarify the best market for Michael's work, he should carefully read several issues of potential candidate publications. It is very important to have a good working knowledge of what each publication is all about. No two are the same; Michael must invest the time to ascertain the differences and send for submission guidelines.

Once Michael discovers a few likely possibilities, he would proceed to clarify very specifically what (tyrannosaurus rexes) he wants to write, who his target audience is, what slant he wants to take, and about how long he wants to make the article. After that, he would put together an outline that more clearly defines what he wants his piece to accomplish. He then has a decision to make. He can proceed to write the whole article or he can see what kind of response he gets to his proposed article by writing a query letter.

A query letter is sent to editors to spark interest in a proposed article idea. (Tip: Smart writers take the time to call the magazine to ask the name of the editor in charge of that subject area and then address the query to him or her). In the letter, Michael needs to state the particulars of his idea *in an engaging fashion* so that it will capture the editor's attention. Editors receive hundreds (even thousands) of these letters every week so Michael's letter must somehow stand out from the rest. Otherwise, he will quickly receive the standard rejection letter, a form letter (or card) stating that the idea "just wasn't right" for the publication (or some other general excuse). This brings to mind another important quality that freelance writers must possess—the ability to withstand rejections. These are sure to be many, but you must have the courage and the inner strength to plunge ahead. To be effective, Michael's query letter should also mention his lifelong study of dinosaurs along with the fact that he teaches creative writing.

Michael could also choose to write the entire article and send that to editors who might be interested in a piece of that nature. Of course, this may better show how talented he is and that the magazine will undoubtedly flourish as a result of his piece, but he has then put many hours into a manuscript that may never sell. However, if you are not an established writer, you may well *have* to produce an entire manuscript to display the full magnitude of your expertise. Once you are established though, well-crafted query letters should suffice. You may even be lucky enough to work strictly "on assignment," meaning that you will be given specific writing topics, slants, story lengths, and deadlines. This way you don't have to create your own story ideas and you know you will be paid for your efforts (unless what you produce is really inferior, heaven forbid, and in that case you may still receive a part of your original fee).

All facets of our society employ freelance writers: newspapers, magazines, associations, nonprofit organizations, business publications, newsletters, public relations firms, department stores, local government, business and industry, television, radio, movies, the list could continue indefinitely. By the very nature of the job description, freelancers are called upon to complete writing projects, often on a seasonal or temporary basis. Rather than hiring staff employees who must be kept busy year-round and who must be given steady salaries and benefits, a large number of companies choose to hire freelance writers.

Freelancers do just about any kind of work that staff writers do, including, but not exclusive to, feature articles, columns, newsletters, book reviews, brochures, public relations writing, speeches, investigative writing, direct mail, sales letters, scientific writing, and educational writing. Most writers who concentrate on poetry, plays, short stories, and fiction and nonfiction books would also be considered freelance writers.

Being a freelance writer requires a heavy dose of self-discipline; after all, there is no one there to tell you that talking on the phone during business hours is taboo or that turning on a television soap opera is probably going to curtail your productivity for that day. You must set your own goals and work toward them at whatever pace your deadlines demand. Establishing good work habits is vital to your success. If you do not, the blank page you started the day with will remain just that way.

Even though freelance writers lead a relatively solitary life, they must be able to work well with others (editors, publishers, art directors, other writers). They must not only be able to express themselves well in print, but also over the phone. Those who possess a pleasing, confident phone presence will ingratiate themselves to others (particularly editors) and fare far better than those who don't come across well. After all, first and foremost, you are selling your most important product—*you*. Secondly, you are selling your writing, something that exists within you, something rather intangible and elusive, especially to those who don't know you.

A freelancer must be very organized and able to juggle a number of projects all at the same time. This may mean performing preliminary research for a book, developing an outline for an article, polishing a short story in its final stages, composing a sales letter, and conducting a series of 12 interviews for an upcoming book all at the same time. Deadlines are not to be missed; if you do it once you may not have the opportunity to do so again. (You probably won't be *given* another opportunity by *that* editor.) In addition, you must keep accurate and up-to-date records of where all your query letters, poems, and manuscripts are; the status of new markets you are trying to breaking into; and all financial transactions (money coming in and money going out) for personal, business, and income tax purposes.

Earnings for freelance writers vary widely. Part-time and beginning writers may earn $1,000 per year or less, but successful part-time writers may receive between $5,000 and $15,000. The rate of payment from magazines varies from $.05 per word to more than $1.00 per word. Large magazines generally pay more than small publications, the latter generally being more receptive to new writers. Experienced writers may sell to national magazines that pay $600 to $4,000 per article. Writers who obtain book contracts usually receive advances against future royalties. In the end, how much these authors earn will depend on the number of books sold and the royalty rate. First-time authors generally receive smaller advances (and probably lower royalty rates) than do established authors like Danielle Steel and Tom Clancy whose publishers know they are proven commodities (best sellers are almost guaranteed).

It is important to be aware that since freelance writers are self-employed, they receive no fringe benefits and must be sure to arrange their own medical insurance.

Competition for freelance work is keen, particularly for beginners. However, when economic times are hard, companies more often use freelancers to fill in the voids left by cuts in staff. For those who are talented, persistent, and knowledgeable, success is possible.

Freelancer Rates

Establishing pay rates is not easy, since there are a number of relevant factors. The client's type and size of business, the nature and magnitude of the project, how quickly it must be finished, and whether you will be paid by the project or by the hour are all considerations. *Writer's Market* suggests that if you are uncertain what to charge, you should begin by charging an hourly rate rather than a flat fee. Establish this rate by determining what an annual salary might be for a staff employee performing the same work. For instance, if you think your prospective client would have to pay an individual $22,000 a year, divide that by 2,000 (approximately 40 hours per week for 50 weeks) and you have a figure of $11 per hour. Next, add 33 percent to cover the costs of fringe benefits (Social Security, unemployment insurance, retirement, and so forth). Then add another dollar-per-hour figure to cover your operating expenses including equipment, supplies, office space, and time spent on business meetings. You may get this figure by adding up one year's expenses and dividing by the number of hours you work on freelance projects each year. Bear in mind that in the beginning your expenses may be considerable, with purchases of computers, fax machines, and the like. Don't add a ridiculous figure that might price you out of everyone's budget. If you wish, you may also add a profit percentage designed for future growth or capital investments. The method of computation is shown here:

$22,000 (salary) ÷ 2,000 (hours) = $11.00 per hour
+ 3.63 (33% for benefits)
+ 2.50 (overhead –$5,000 expenses per year)
+ 1.10 (10% profit margin)
$18.23 per hour charge

Suggested Freelance Fees

Advertising, Copywriting, and Public relations

Advertising copywriting: $20 to $100 per hour. Flat fee per ad could range from $100 and up per page.

Book jacket copywriting: From $100–$600 for front jacket cover plus flaps and back jacket copy.

Brochures: $20 to $600 per published page or $100 to $7,500 and up per project.

Copyediting for advertising: $25 per hour.

Copywriting for book club catalogs: $85 to $200.

Flyer: $50 and up.

Press release: 1 to 3 pages, $25 to $500.

Print advertisement: $200 per project.

Product literature: $60 per hour; $100 to $300 per page.

Proofreading corporate publications: $15 to $25 per hour.

Public relations for business: $250 to $600 per day.

Public relations for libraries: $5 to $35 per hour and up.

Public relations for politicians: Small-town, state campaigns, $10 to $50 per hour; other campaigns, $25 to $100 per hour up to 10 percent of budget.

Radio advertising copy: $20 to $100 per script; larger cities, $250 to $400 per week.

Speech, editing, and evaluation: $18 per hour and up.

Speech for government official: $4,000 for 20 minutes.

Speech for local political candidate: $250 for 15 minutes; for statewide candidate, $375 to $500.

Speechwriting (general): $20 to $75 per hour.

Trade journal ad copywriting: $250 to $500.

TV commercial: $60 to $75 per finished minute.

Audiovisuals and Electronic Communications

Audiocassette scripts: $10 to $50 per scripted minute.

Book summaries for film producers: $50 to $100 per book. (Note: You must live in the area to secure this work.)

Copyediting audiovisuals; $20 per hour.

Radio continuity writing: $5 per page to $150 per week, part time.

Radio documentaries: $258 for 60 minutes, local station.

Radio editorials: $10 to $30 for 90-second to 2-minute spots.

Radio interviews: For National Public Radio, up to 3 minutes, $25; 3 to 10 minutes, $40 to $75; 10 to 60 minutes, $125 and up.

Screenwriting: $6,000 and up per project.

Slide presentation: Including visual formats plus audio, $150 to $600 for 10 to 15 minutes.

TV information scripts: Short 5- to 10-minute scripts for local cable TV stations, $10 to $15 per hour.

TV news story: $16 to $25.

TV scripts: 60 minutes; network prime time, Writers Guild Rates; $14,048; 30 minutes, $10,414.

Books

Book summaries for book clubs: $50 to $100 per book.

Copyediting: $10 to $35 per hour.

Ghostwriting, as told to: Author gets full advance and 50 percent of author's royalties; subject gets 50 percent. Hourly rate for those self-publishing, $25 to $50 per hour.

Proofreading: $12 to $25 per hour and up.

Research for writers or book publishers: $15 to $40 per hour.

Textbook copyediting: $15 to $20 per hour.

Textbook editing: $15 to $30 per hour.

Business and Technical Writing

Annual reports: $20 to $35 per hour and up.

Associations: $15 to $20 per hour and up. Flat fee such as $550 for 1,000 to 2,000-word magazine article.

Business booklets, announcement brochures: Writing and editing, $100 to $1,000.

Business content editing: $20 to $35 per hour.

Business facilities brochure: 12 to 16 pages, $1,000 to $4,000.

Business letters: $100 to $500.

Business writing: $25 to $60 per hour.

Business writing seminars: $250 to $400 per day.

Commercial reports: $6 to $10 per page; $5 to $20 per short report.

Company newsletters and in-house publications: Writing and editing 2 to 4 pages, $200 to $500; 4 to 8 pages, $500 to $1,000. Writing, $20 to $60 per hour; editing, $15 to $40 per hour.

Corporate comedy: Half-hour show, $300 to $800.

Financial corporation presentation: 20 to 30 minutes; $1,500 to $4,500.

Ghostwriting, general: $25 to $100 per hour.

Handbooks: $50 to $100 per hour; $25 per hour for nonprofit.

Job application letters: $20 to $40.

Newsletters, editing: $50 to $500 per issue.

Newsletter writing: $500 to $5,000 per issue.

Proofreading: $15 to $50 per hour.

Resume writing: $25 to $500 per resume.

Science writing: For newspapers, $150 to $600; magazines, $2,000 to $5,000; encyclopedias, $1 per line; professional publications, $500 to $1,500 for 1,500 to 3,000 words.

Software manual writing: $35 to $50 per hour for research and writing.

Technical editing: $15 to $60 per hour.

Technical writing: $35 to $75 per hour.

Photo brochures: $700 to $15,000 for photos and writing.

Photography: $5 to $150 per black and white photo; $10 to $300 per color photo.

Educational and Literary Services

Lectures at national conventions by well-known authors: $2,500 to $20,000 and up.

Lectures at regional writers' conferences: $300 and up.

Lectures to local librarians or teachers: $50 to $100.

Lectures to school classes: $25 to $75; $150 to $250 per day.

Readings by poets, fiction writers: $25 to $600.

Teaching adult education course: $10 to $60 per class hour.

Teaching business writing to company employees: $60 per hour.

Teaching college course or seminar: $15 to $70 per hour of instruction.

Teaching elementary and middle school teachers how to teach writing to students: $75 to $120 for a 1½ hour session.

Writer-in-schools: Arts council program, $130 per day.

Writer's workshop: Lecturing and conducting seminar, $50 to $150 per hour.

Writing for scholarly journals: $75 per hour.

Magazines and Trade Journals

Book reviews: $50 to $300.

Copyediting: $13 to $30 per hour.

Editing: General, $25 to $500 per day or $250 to $2,000 per issue; religious publications, $15 to $30 per hour.

Fact checking: $17 to $25 per hour.

Feature articles: Anywhere from 10 cents to $4 per word or $200 to $2,000 per 2,000-word article.

Ghostwriting articles (general): Up to $2 per word.

Magazine column: 200 words, $40; 800 words, $400; sometimes $1 per word; larger circulation magazines may pay more.

Stringing: 20 cents to $1 per word based on circulation; sometimes $1 per column inch.

Trade journal feature article: For business client, $400 to $1,000; also, $1 per word.

Newspapers

Ads for small business: $25 per small, one-column ad; or $10 per hour.

Book reviews: For small newspapers, byline and the book only; for larger publications, $35 to $200.

Column, local: $10 to $20 for a weekly; $15 to $30 for dailies of 4,000 to 6,000; $30 to $50 for 7,000 to 10,000 dailies, to $100 and up.

Feature: $25 to $35 per article for a weekly; $40 to $500 for a daily; also 10 cents to 20 cents per word.

Stringing: Sometimes flat rate of $20 to $35 to cover meeting and write article.

Miscellaneous

Comedy writing for night club entertainers: Gags only, $5 to $25 each; routines, $100 to $1,000 per minute.

Craft ideas with instructions: $50 to $200 per project.

Greeting card verse: $25 to $300 per idea.

PLAYWRIGHTS

Playwrights write the scripts for stage plays that will be performed by actors in university theater divisions, community theaters, Broadway and off-Broadway theaters, and radio and television productions. Dialogue, action, and visual dynamics are important qualities that playwrights must use to their best advantage in all of their works.

Playwrights usually begin their careers in local theaters. Here they learn the basics of what is effective, how a production budget is allocated, and how to stage a scene. Writing for a local theater means developing a play with few characters, sparse props, and simple lighting demands. After building a successful reputation at this level, playwrights may move on to larger audiences.

SCREENWRITERS

Assigned the task of writing scripts for films (or television), screenwriters, more than other writers, work on assignment for motion picture studios. Often they are contracted to adapt books or plays for movies (or television), although they may also submit original screenplays.

Since the visual impact is so important in this medium, screenwriters usually write detailed visual directions in addition to the dialogue. Some of the most poignant scenes may contain no dialogue at all.

Competition is very keen for both playwrights and screenwriters.

POETS

A miniscule number of people make their living writing poetry but many are poets in addition to engaging in other careers or other forms of writing.

Poetry styles vary widely, but often poets employ imagery, similes, metaphors, and other dramatic devices to tell their stories. Some poets use traditional rhyme and meter, whereas others write in free verse (poetry that often has meter, but no rhyme).

HUMORISTS

Humorists write funny or clever lines for stories that will appear in magazines or books; they also provide material for performers. These individuals have an up-to-date understanding of what's going on in the world, a humorous approach to life, and a precise sense of timing.

SONGWRITERS, COMPOSERS, LYRICISTS, AND LIBRETTISTS

Some songwriters create both the music and the lyrics, others do only one or the other. Sometimes lyricists and composers work together to create songs. Rogers and Hammerstein were famous for this type of successful arrangement. Some composers may write only classical music, such as symphonies, while others write for the Broadway stage or popular music. The music for radio and television commercials is written by composers, as are the themes and background music for movies and television shows. Librettists write the words for operas, musical plays, or long choral works, usually adapting their writing to already existing music. They may also write descriptions of the cast, plot summaries, and stage directions and descriptions. Composers often comment that they write their music to express a feeling or tell a story just as poets and other types of writers do.

BOOK REVIEWERS/CRITICS

Book reviewers are responsible for analyzing new books to see how they measure up to literary standards and mass appeal. Some critics are full-time employees of newspapers, magazines, television, or radio; others operate in a freelance capacity. Since there are very few reviewers who earn a full-time livelihood, book reviewers often have written (and/or are writing) books of their own.

Obviously, book reviewers msut be cognizant of the elements that are inherent in quality writing: strong characterizations, interesting and unique plotting, satisfactory and sensible conclusions, to name a few. They must also be aware of public trends and likes and dislikes. In writing their review, they will relate what the book is about and point out its strengths and weaknesses.

Critics may play an important role in the sales of a book. Readers are apt to believe what they see in print; therefore, it is a profitable financial boon to a new book to receive a favorable review, especially from a recognized critic.

GHOSTWRITERS

Ghostwriters may be asked to write anything from an article or short story to an entire book, usually by individuals who do not have the time or expertise to do the writing. The writers generally get no credit for doing the work; it appears as if the employer did the writing and his or her name is the one that appears as the author. Autobiographies of famous people are often ghostwritten.

LITERARY AGENTS

Literary agents represent clients who wish to sell their work to publishers, producers, or other employers. These individuals must have experience as editors (and perhaps writers) to be able to discern the quality of a manuscript. Since they work strictly on a commission basis, they are not interested in allying themselves with unprofessional writers whose work does not show talent and polish. Sometimes they will see promise in a writer's work and make specific suggestions about how the work could be improved.

Agents serve authors, musicians, playwrights, and other types of writers (not usually poets, short-story writers, or article writers). By submitting manuscripts, writers hope agents will be impressed enough to represent them. Publishers are more likely to consider works from agents; in fact, some publishers don't consider work that is not submitted by an agent. For their commission, agents arrange contracts and advise and guide their clients' careers.

With their knowledge of what publishers, movie studios, and television producers are seeking, they have a better idea of where (and to whom) to send manuscripts. With their expertise in the nuances of the business, they are able to get a better deal for their clients; perhaps a bigger advance, higher royalty, or preservation of movie rights. Many writers are happy to have agents; ultimately, it keeps relationships with editors nonadversarial and frees the writers to do what they love most—write.

Part Three
Preparing for a Career in Journalism

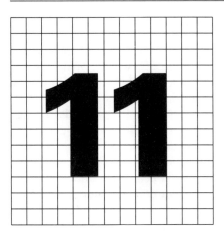

EDUCATIONAL BACKGROUND

The quality of a person's life is in direct proportion to their commitment to excellence, regardless of their chosen field of endeavor.

—Vince Lombardi

Paving a path to excellence requires you to prepare yourself so that you are always ready to take the next step. What preparation will you need for a career in journalism?

If you are in high school, hopefully you've embarked on a course of study designed for college-bound students. This probably includes four years of English, in addition to several years of history, social studies, business courses, computer literacy, natural sciences, math, and a foreign language. Additional coursework in literature, journalism, drama, art, and photography are also pluses. The courses you've taken, your test scores, your grade point average, and your class rank will be important in determining what colleges or universities will accept you to their programs.

WHERE DO YOU BEGIN?

With hundreds of institutions to choose from, how do you decide where to go and what your educational plan should be? Several factors should be taken into consideration:

Location
Difficulty of admittance
Program major
Scholarship availability
Tuition and living costs

Other factors students take into consideration are the reputation of the college or university (department and program), quality of instruction, school size, makeup of the student body, their familiarity with the school, where their friends and family are going or have attended, and other social factors.

THE PATH TO THE WORLD OF JOURNALISM

Once you've decided to follow your heart into the world of journalism, is it best to get a degree in journalism? This is a subject for debate. Many newspaper publishing executives, for instance, believe a journalism degree is the most important consideration in assessing a job applicant. Others indicate a preference for reporters and editors with broad liberal arts backgrounds. Though there is no universal agreement on this, the consensus seems to be that taking liberal arts courses in combination with journalism courses is a winning combination for print journalists. For broadcast journalists, experts recommend a major in political science, history, government, or economics with a minor in journalism (broadcast journalism, if possible); a double major in broadcast journalism and economics, history, or the like; or a major in broadcast journalism with strong electives in history, government, and economics.

Is it necessary to get an advanced degree? There is no universal agreement on this either, but advanced degrees, though usually not required, are certainly considered an asset for the job seeker. One notable exception applies if you plan to specialize in a designated area, such as political or medical journalism. If this is the case, a master's degree is highly desirable.

Those majoring in journalism will find themselves immersed in a broad spectrum of general courses that merge with classes in news writing, editing, and photography. About ten of the required courses, translating to about 25 percent of the curriculum, are journalism subjects. Thirty other courses (about 75 percent of the overall curriculum) are added to fill out the program. Figure 11.1 illustrates this breakdown of classes. These other classes provide a broad base of learning in both the arts and the sciences. Though titles may differ, most schools require classes such as the following to provide the core curriculum:

Introduction to Journalism: Print Media
History of Journalism
Law and Communications
Beginning Reporting
Beginning Editing
Photojournalism

Advanced skills will be emphasized through the following courses: feature writing, investigative reporting, editorial writing, advanced reporting, graphics, advanced editing, and media management. Other classes may include broadcast journalism, communications and public opinion, communications and popular culture, broadcast documentary form, magazine article writing, graphic arts, broadcast news production, radio, television writing and production, business communications, travel writing, science writing, and column writing.

All course work culminates in the long-awaited *internship,* where budding journalists are placed in an advanced in-service training with a professional publication, a broadcast station, or a public relations agency. Everyone agrees that this experience is invaluable to the student, not only in

Figure 11.1 Courses to prepare you for your Journalism Career

25% JOURNALISM CLASSES
- REPORTING
- HISTORY OF JOURNALISM
- PHOTOJOURNALISM
- ETHICS AND LAW
- WRITING

75% LIBERAL ARTS CLASSES
- ENGLISH
- HISTORY
- POLITICAL SCIENCE
- NATURAL SCIENCEs
  BIOLOGY
  CHEMISTRY
- MATH
- SOCIOLOGY
- ECONOMICS

terms of the knowledge and practical wisdom gained, but also in terms of its desirability to employers. Many feel that internships are a necessity for everyone prior to being hired as full-time journalists.

COLLEGE BOUND

With the vast number of colleges and universities that offer journalism programs, making a choice can indeed be a voluminous task. How can the huge number of institutions be evaluated? The Accrediting Council on Education in Journalism and Mass Communications, certified by the U.S. Office of Education, has done it for you in its *Accredited Journalism and Mass Communications Education,* published every year. Schools included in this list have met stringent standards of integrity, quality, and performance.

The following is their list for 1993–1994 with degrees offered and available scholarships noted.

Alabama
University of Alabama
College of Communication
P.O. Box 870172
Tuscaloosa, AL 35487-0172

Edward Mullins, Dean
B.A. Communication; M.A. Communication.
Majors/Sequences: Journalism, Advertising/Public Relations,
Telecommunication and Film Communication, Speech Com-
munication, Photojournalism, Magazine.
Number of scholarships for journalism/mass communication
students: 35, for a total of $35,620; includes five minority
scholarships totaling $1,000.

Alaska
University of Alaska–Anchorage
Department of Journalism and Public Communications
3211 Providence Drive
Anchorage, AK 99508
Dr. Sylvia Broady, Chair
B.A. Journalism.
Majors/Sequences: News–Editorial, Public Relations, Adver-
tising, Photojournalism, Telecommunications, General Com-
munications.
Number of scholarships for journalism/mass communication
students: 4, for a total of $4,000; includes 3 minority scholar-
ships for $3,000.

University of Alaska Fairbanks
Department of Journalism Broadcasting
18 Bunnell
Fairbanks, AK 99775-0940
Jerry Brigham, Head
B.A. Journalism.
Majors/Sequences: News–Editorial, Broadcast Journalism.
Number of scholarships for journalism/mass communication
students: 10, for a total of $7,000; includes 2 minority scholar-
ships totaling $2,000.

Arizona
Arizona State University
Walter Cronkite School of Journalism and Telecommunication
Tempe, AZ 85287-1305
Dr. Douglas A. Anderson, Director
B.A. Journalism; B.A. Broadcasting; M.M.C. Mass
Communication.
Majors/Sequences: Print Journalism, Public Relations, Photo-
journalism, Telecommunication Management, Broadcast
Journalism.
Number of scholarships for journalism/mass communication
students: 60, for a total of $50,100; includes 12 minority

scholarships totaling $10,000 and 8 graduate scholarships totaling $8,000.

University of Arizona
Department of Journalism
Tucson, AZ 85721
Professor Jim Patten, Head
B.A. Journalism; M.A. Journalism.
Majors/Sequences: News–Editorial, Magazine, Community
Journalism, Public Information, Photojournalism.
Number of scholarships for journalism/mass communication
students: 30, for a total of $25,000; includes 5 minority
scholarships totaling $5,000.

Arkansas
Arkansas State University
Department of Journalism
State University, AR 72467
Joel Gambill, Chair
B.S. Journalism; M.S. Journalism, M.C. Journalism.
Majors/Sequences: News–Editorial, Public Relations, Advertising, Photojournalism, Community Journalism, Broadcast
News, Broadcast Production, Broadcast Advertising and
Sales.
Number of scholarships for journalism/mass communication
students: 21, for a total of $77,950; includes 5 minority scholarships totaling $5,000 and 7 graduate scholarships totaling
$49,000.

University of Arkansas
Department of Journalism
Fayetteville, AR 72701-1201
Dr. Patsy Watkins, Chair
B.A. Journalism; M.A. Journalism.
Majors/Sequences: News–Editorial, Broadcast Journalism,
Advertising, Public Relations, Magazine, Photography.
Number of scholarships for journalism/mass communication
students: 31, for a total of $25,400; includes 2 minority scholarships totaling $2,500 and 2 graduate scholarships totaling
$2,000.

University of Arkansas
Department of Journalism
2801 S. University
Little Rock, AR 72204
Dr. E.J. Friendlander, Chair
B.A. Journalism; M.A. Journalism.
Majors/Sequences: News–Editorial, Broadcast Journalism,

Public Information, Professional and Technical Writing.
Number of scholarships for journalism/mass communication
students: 16, for a total of $14,000.

California

California State University
Department of Mass Communication and Journalism
Fresno, CA 93740-0010
R.C. Adams, Chair
B.A. Mass Communication and Journalism; M.A. Mass Com-
munication.
Majors/Sequences: News–Editorial, Advertising, Public Rela-
tions, Radio–TV News Communication, Photo-
communications.
Number of scholarships for journalism/mass communication
students: 24, for a total of $19,000; includes 10 minority
scholarships totaling $10,000.

California State University
Department of Communications
P.O. Box 34080
Fullerton, CA 92634-9480
Dr. Terry Hynes, Chair
B.A. Communications; M.A. Communications.
Majors/Sequences: Advertising, Print and Broadcast Journal-
ism, Photocommunications, Public Relations, Film.
Number of scholarships for journalism/mass communication
students: 10, for a total of $8,800; includes 1 graduate scholar-
ship totaling $4,000.

California State University, Long Beach
Department of Journalism
1250 Bellflower Blvd.
Long Beach, CA 90840
William A. Mulligan, Chair
B.A. Journalism.
Majors/Sequences: News–Editorial, Public Relations, Maga-
zine, Broadcast Journalism, Photojournalism, Secondary
School Teaching.
Number of scholarships for journalism/mass communication
students: 10, for a total of $11,700; includes 1 minority schol-
arship totaling $1,000.

California State University
Department of Journalism
Northridge, CA 91330
Dr. Tom Reilly, Chair

B.A. Journalism; M.A. Mass Communication.
Major/Sequence: News–Editorial.
Number of scholarships for journalism/mass communication students: 12, for a total of $14,200; includes 4 graduate scholarships totaling $12,000.

Humboldt State University
Department of Journalism
Arcata, CA 95521
Professor Mark A. Larson, Chair
B.A. Journalism.
Majors/Sequences: News–Editorial, Public Relations, Broadcast News, Media Studies.
Number of scholarships for journalism/mass communication students: 7, for a total of $3,000.

San Diego State University
Department of Journalism
San Diego, CA 92182
Dr. Glen Broom, Chair
B.A. Journalism; M.S. Mass Communications.
Majors/Sequences: News–Editorial, Advertising, Public Relations, Radio–TV News.
Number of scholarships for journalism/mass communication students: 18, for a total of $10,300. Includes 6 minority scholarships, totaling $2,500. Includes 3 graduate scholarships, totaling $1,500.

San Francisco State University
Department of Journalism
1600 Holloway Avenue
San Francisco, CA 94132
Professor Betty Medsger, Chair
B.A. Journalism; M.A. Interdisciplinary Special Masters.
Majors/Sequences: News–Editorial, Magazine, Photojournalism.
Number of scholarships for journalism/mass communication students: 8, for a total of $11,500.

San Jose State University
School of Journalism and Mass Communications
San Jose, CA 95192-0055
Dr. Kenneth Blase, Director
B.S. Journalism; B.S. Advertising; B.S. Public Relations; M.S. Mass Communications.
Majors/Sequences: Reporting and Editing, Photojournalism, Advertising, Public Relations, Radio–TV Journalism, Magazine/Media Writing and Production.

Number of scholarships for journalism/mass communication students: 18, for a total of $10,000.

University of California
Graduate School of Journalism
121 North Gate Hall
Berkeley, CA 94720
Professor Tom Goldstein, Dean
M.J. Journalism.
Majors/Sequences: News–Editorial (graduate), Television News (graduate).
Number of scholarships for journalism/mass communication students: 18, for a total of $80,000.

Colorado
Colorado State University
Department of Technical Journalism
Fort Collins, CO 80523
Dr. James K. VanLeuven, Chair
B.A. Technical Journalism; B.A. Agricultural/Natural Resources Journalism; M.S. Technical Communication.
Majors/Sequences: Electronic Reporting, News–Editorial, Public Relations, Technical–Specialized, Agricultural/Natural Resources Journalism.
Number of scholarships for journalism/mass communication students: 10, for a total of $7,000.

University of Colorado
School of Journalism and Mass Communication
Campus Box 287
Boulder, CO 80309
Dr. Willard D. Rowland Jr., Dean
B.S. Journalism; M.A. Journalism.
Majors/Sequences: News–Editorial, Advertising, Broadcast Production Management, Broadcast News.
Number of scholarships for journalism/mass communication students: 18, for a total of $16,400.

District of Columbia
Howard University
Department of Journalism
Washington, DC 20059
Dr. Clint C. Wilson II, Chair
B.A. Journalism
Department of Radio–TV–Film
Bishetta Merritt, Chair
B.A. Broadcast Production and Telecommunications Management.

Majors/Sequences: News–Editorial, Broadcast News, Public Relations, Advertising.
Number of scholarships for journalism/mass communication students: 25, for a total of $150,000.

The American University
School of Communication
Washington, DC 20016-8017
Sanford Ungar, Dean
B.A. Communication–Journalism; B.A. Communication–Public Communication; B.A. Communication–Visual Media; M.A. Journalism and Public Affairs; M.A. Public Communication; M.A. Film and Video.
Major Sequences: Broadcast Journalism, Print Journalism, Public Communication, Visual Media, Journalism and Public Affairs (Broadcast or Print, graduate), Film and Video (graduate), Public Communication (graduate).
Number of scholarships for journalism/mass communication students: 3, for a total of $60,000.

Florida
Florida A&M University
Division of Journalism
Tallahassee, FL 32307
James E. Hawkins, Director
B.S.J. Journalism.
Majors/Sequences: Newspaper Journalism, Broadcast Journalism, Public Relations, Magazine, Photography and Graphic Design.
Number of scholarships for journalism/mass communication students: 32, for a total of $40,000; includes 24 minority scholarships totaling $30,000.

Florida International University
School of Journalism and Mass Communication
North Miami, FL 33181
Dr. J. Arthur Heise, Dean
B.S. Communication; M.S. Mass Communication.
Majors/Sequences: Print Journalism, Broadcast Journalism, Public Relations, Broadcasting (Production, Management), Advertising.
Number of scholarships for journalism/mass communication students: 19, for a total of $17,850; includes 18 minority scholarships totaling $16,850.

University of Florida
College of Journalism and Communications

Gainesville, FL 32611-2084
Ralph Lowenstein, Dean
B.S. Telecommunication; B.S. Public Relations; M.A. Mass
Communication.
Majors/Sequences: News–Editorial, Advertising, Telecommunication, Public Relations, Technical Communications, Magazines, Photojournalism.
Number of scholarships for journalism/mass communication
students: 125, for a total of $160,000; includes 30 minority
scholarships totaling $60,000 and 12 graduate fellowships to-
taling $30,000.

University of Miami
School of Communication
Coral Gables, FL 33124-2030
Edward J. Pfister, Dean
B.S.; B.F.A.; M.A.; M.F.A.

University of South Florida
School of Mass Communications
4202 E. Fowler–C151040
Tampa, FL 33620
Dr. Donna Dickerson, Director
B.A. Mass Communications; M.A. Mass Communications.
Major Sequences: News–Editorial, Advertising, Magazine
Journalism, Public Relations, Broadcast News, Visual Com-
munications, Broadcast Programming and Production.
Number of scholarships for journalism/mass communication
students: 15, for a total of $9,000; includes 4 minority scholar-
ships totaling $3,000.

University of West Florida
Department of Communication Arts
11000 University Parkway
Pensacola, FL 32514-5751
Dr. Churchill L. Roberts, Chair
Majors/Sequences: News–Editorial, Broadcast Journalism,
Public Relations/Advertising, Radio–Television–Film.
Number of scholarships for journalism/mass communication
students: 6, for a total of $2,000.

Georgia
University of Georgia
Henry W. Grady College of Journalism and Mass
Communication
Athens, GA 30602
J. Thomas Russell, Dean

A.B.J. Journalism; M.A. Journalism; M.A. Mass
Communication.

Hawaii

University of Hawaii at Manoa
Department of Journalism
Honolulu, HI 96822
Lowell D. Frazier, Chair
Major Sequences: News–Editorial, Broadcast Journalism,
Public Relations.
Number of scholarships for journalism/mass communication
students: 27, for a total of $30,700.

Illinois

Eastern Illinois University
Department of Journalism
Charleston, IL 61920
John David Reed, Chair
B.A. Journalism.
Majors/Sequences: News–Editorial, Public Relations Adver-
tising, Broadcast News, Magazine, Photography.
Number of scholarships for journalism/mass communication
students: 42, for a total of $22,044; includes 3 minority schol-
arships totaling $1,650.

Northern Illinois University
Department of Journalism
DeKalb, IL 60115
Dr. Daniel Riffe, Chair
B.A. Journalism; B.S. Journalism; M.A. Journalism.
Majors/Sequences: News–Editorial, Broadcast News, Public
Relations, Photojournalism.
Number of scholarships for journalism/mass communication
students: 14, for a total of $9,600; includes 5 minority scholar-
ships totaling $4,000 and 3 graduate scholarships totaling
$2,500.

Northwestern University
Medill School of Journalism
Fisk Hall
Evanston, IL 60208
Michael C. Janeway, Dean
B.S.J. Journalism; M.S.A. Integrated Advertising/Marketing
Communications; M.S.J. Journalism.
Majors/Sequences: News–Editorial (undergraduate), Maga-
zine, Advertising, TV News, Advertising, Corporate Public
Relations, Direct Mailing (graduate).

Number of scholarships for journalism/mass communication students: 1, for a total of $24,000; includes 1 minority scholarship for a graduate editorial student, totaling $24,000.

Southern Illinois University at Carbondale
School of Journalism
Carbondale, IL 62901
Dr. Walter Jaehnig, Director
B.S. Journalism; M.A. Journalism; M.S. Journalism.
Majors/Sequences: News–Editorial, Advertising.
Number of scholarships for journalism/mass communication students: 47, for a total of $82,500; includes 17 graduate scholarships totaling $68,000.

University of Illinois at Urbana–Champaign
College of Communications
810 S. Wright St.
Urbana, IL 61801
Kim Rotzell, Dean
B.S. Advertising; B.S. Media Studies; B.S. Journalism, including Broadcast Journalism; M.S. Advertising; M.S. Journalism, including Broadcast Journalism.
Majors/Sequences: News–Editorial, Advertising, Broadcast News, Media Studies.
Number of scholarships for journalism/mass communication students: 50, for a total of $65,000; includes 15 graduate scholarships totaling $45,000.

Indiana
Ball State University
Department of Journalism
Muncie, IN 47306
Dr. Earl L. Conn, Chair
B.A. Journalism; B.S. Journalism; M.A. Journalism; M.A. Public Relations.
Majors/Sequences: News–Editorial, Newspaper Advertising, Photojournalism, Magazine Journalism, Secondary School Journalism, Public Relations, Journalism Graphics.
Number of scholarships for journalism/mass communication students: 33, for a total of $19,550; includes 2 minority scholarships totaling $2,000 and 1 graduate scholarship totaling $500.

Indiana University
School of Journalism and Mass Communication
Bloomington, IN 47405

Dr. Trevor R. Brown, Dean
B.A.J.; M.A. Professional; M.A. Research.
Majors/Sequences: News–Editorial, Broadcast News, Photojournalism, Magazine, Public Relations, Advertising, Education, Professional Graduate.
Number of scholarships for journalism/mass communication
students: 95, for a total of $147,500; includes graduate schol-
arships totaling $71,750.

Iowa
Drake University
School of Journalism and Mass Communication
Des Moines, IA 50311
Louis J. Wolter, Acting Dean
B.A. Journalism and Mass Communication; M.A. Mass
Communication.
Majors/Sequences: News–Editorial, Creative Advertising, Ad-
vertising Management, Broadcast News, Magazine, Public
Relations, Radio–Television Management and Production,
Journalism Teaching.
Number of scholarships for journalism/mass communication
students: 12, for a total of $39,745.

Iowa State University of Science and Technology
Department of Journalism and Mass Communication
Ames, IA 50011
Dr. J. Thomas Emmerson, Chair
B.A. Journalism and Mass Communication, including Elec-
tronic Media Studies; B.A. Advertising; B.S. Journalism and
Mass Communication; M.S. Journalism and Mass
Communication.
Majors/Sequences: News–Editorial, Electronic Media Studies
(Broadcast News/Production), Advertising, Agricultural Jour-
nalism, Family and Consumer Journalism, General Journal-
ism, Science Writing, Engineering Journalism, Public
Relations, Magazine, Visual Communication.
Number of scholarships for journalism/mass communication
students: 49, for a total of $30,500; includes 4 to 5 minority
scholarships totaling $2,500 to $3,000.

University of Iowa
School of Journalism and Mass Communication
Iowa City, IA 52242
Dr. Kenneth Starck, Director
B.A. Journalism; B.S. Journalism; M.A. Professional.
Majors/Sequences: News–Editorial, Magazine, Broadcast
Journalism, Public Relations, Photography.

Number of scholarships for journalism/mass communication students: 69, for a total of $49,700; includes 11 graduate scholarships totaling $5,000.

Kansas

Kansas State University
A.Q. Miller School of Journalism and Mass Communications
Manhattan, KS 66506
Dr. Carol Oukrop, Director
B.A. Journalism; B.S. Journalism; M.S. Mass Communication.
Majors/Sequences: News–Editorial, Radio–TV, Public Relations, Advertising.
Number of scholarships for journalism/mass communication students: 25, for a total of $45,000; includes 2 to 3 minority scholarships totaling $2,500 and 2 graduate scholarships totaling $5,000.

University of Kansas
William Allen White School of Journalism and Mass Communications
Lawrence, KS 66045
Mike Kautsch, Dean
B.S. Journalism; M.S. Journalism.
Majors/Sequences: News (Community Journalism, Newspaper Journalism, Photojournalism, Business Communications), Advertising, Magazine, Radio–TV.
Number of scholarships for journalism/mass communication students: 70, for a total of $84,000; includes 7 minority scholarships totaling $14,000 and 3 graduate scholarships totaling $12,500.

Kentucky

Murray State University
Department of Journalism and Radio–TV
Box 2456
University Station
Murray, KY 42071
Dr. Robert H. McGaughey III, Chair
B.A. or B.S. Journalism, Advertising, Public Relations and Radio–TV; M.A.; M.S.
Majors/Sequences: News–Editorial, Advertising, Public Relations, Radio–Television.
Number of scholarships for journalism/mass communication students: 18, for a total of $11,000; includes 3 minority scholarships totaling $1,500 and 1 graduate scholarship totaling $4,500.

Western Kentucky University
Department of Journalism
Bowling Green, KY 42101
Jo-Ann Huff Albers, Head
B.A. Public Relations; B.A. Advertising; B.A. Photojournalism; B.A. Print Journalism
Majors/Sequences: News–Editorial, Public Relations, Photojournalism, Advertising.
Number of scholarships for journalism/mass communication students: 26, for a total of $14,610; includes 3 minority scholarships totaling $1,500.

University of Kentucky
School of Journalism and Telecommunications
Lexington, KY 40506
Roy L. Moore, Acting Director
B.A. Journalism; B.S. Journalism.
Majors/Sequences: General Editorial, Advertising.
Number of scholarships for journalism/mass communication students: 17, for a total of $10,850; includes 5 minority scholarships totaling $3,000.

Louisiana

Grambling State University
Department of Mass Communication
Grambling, LA 71245
Dr. Rama Tunuguntla, Head
B.A. Mass Communication.
Majors/Sequences: News–Editorial, Technical Writing, Visual Communication, Public Relations, Broadcasting.

Louisiana State University
Manship School of Mass Communication
Baton Rouge, LA 70803
John Maxwell Hamilton, Director
B.A.M.C.; M.M.C.
Majors/Sequences: News–Editorial, Advertising, Broadcast Journalism, Journalism (graduate).
Number of scholarships for journalism/mass communication students: 29, for a total of $46,000; includes 5 minority scholarships totaling $2,500 and 3 graduate fellowships totaling $30,000.

Maryland
University of Maryland
College of Journalism
College Park, MD 20742

Professor Reese Cleghorn, Dean
B.A. Journalism; M.A. Journalism.
Majors/Sequences: News–Editorial (News Magazine), Public
Relations, Advertising, Broadcast News.
Number of scholarships for journalism/mass communication
students: 32, for a total of $216,200; includes 7 minority
scholarships totaling $20,500 and 16 graduate scholarships to-
taling $169,000.

Michigan
Michigan State University
School of Journalism
East Lansing, MI 48824-1212
Stan Soffin, Director
B.A. Journalism; M.A. Journalism.
Majors/Sequences: News–Editorial, Public Relations,
Radio–TV News, Photojournalism, Magazine, Advertising.
Number of scholarships for journalism/mass communication
students: 20, for a total of $55,000; includes 6 minority schol-
arships totaling $23,490 and 5 graduate scholarships totaling
$25,000.

Minnesota
St. Cloud State University
Department of Mass Communications
St. Cloud, MN 56301-4498
Amde-Michael Habte, Chair
B.S. Mass Communications; M.S. Communication
Management.
Majors/Sequences: Advertising, News–Editorial, Broadcasting,
Public Relations, Communication Management (graduate).
Number of scholarships for journalism/mass communication
students: 17, for a total of $7,340; includes 1 minority scholar-
ship totaling $400.

University of Minnesota
School of Journalism and Mass Communication
Minneapolis, MN 55455-0418
Professor Daniel Wackman, Director
B.A. Journalism–Professional Program; B.A.
Journalism–Mass Communication Program; M.A. Mass
Communication.
Majors/Sequences: News–Editorial, Advertising, Broadcast
Journalism, Visual Communication, Magazine, Photography,
Public Relations, Mass Communication.
Number of scholarships for journalism/mass communication
students: 60, for a total of $104,000; includes 1 minority

scholarship totaling $1,000 and 25 graduate scholarships totaling $55,000.

Mississippi
Jackson State University
Department of Mass Communications
Jackson, MS 39217
Doris E. Saunders, Chair
B.S. Mass Communications.
Majors/Sequences: News–Editorial, Public Relations, Advertising, Broadcast Production, Broadcast Journalism.

University of Southern Mississippi
Department of Journalism
Hattiesburg, MS 39406-5121
Arthur Kaul, Chair
B.A. Journalism; B.A. Advertising.

University of Mississippi
Department of Journalism
University, MS 38677
Dr. Don Sneed, Chair
B.A. Journalism; B.S.J. Journalism; M.A. Journalism.
Majors/Sequences: News–Editorial, Broadcast Journalism, Journalism/Advertising.
Number of scholarships for journalism/mass communication students; 25, for a total of $27,000; includes 3 minority scholarships totaling $2,500 and 5 graduate scholarships for print students totaling $15,000.

Missouri
University of Missouri–Columbia
School of Journalism
Box 838
Columbia, MO 62505
Dean Mills, Dean
B.J. Journalism; M.A. Journalism.
Majors/Sequences: News–Editorial, Advertising, Magazine, Broadcast News, Photojournalism, Professional Program (graduate).
Number of scholarships for journalism/mass communication students: 200, for a total of $200,000; includes 25 minority scholarships totaling $20,000 and 100 graduate scholarships totaling $105,000.

Montana
The University of Montana
School of Journalism

Missoula, MT 59812
Joe Durso, Jr., Acting Dean
B.A. Journalism; B.A. Radio–Television; M.A. Journalism.
Majors/Sequences: News–Editorial, Radio–TV (general).
Number of scholarships for journalism/mass communication
students: 40, for a total of $25,250; includes 5 minority schol-
arships totaling $5,000.

Nebraska
University of Nebraska
College of Journalism
Lincoln, NE 68558-0127
Dr. Will Norton, Dean
B.J. Journalism; M.A. Journalism.
Majors/Sequences: Advertising, News–Editorial, Broadcasting
(general), Professional Program (graduate).
Number of scholarships for journalism/mass communication
students: 54, for a total of $65,000; includes 10 minority
scholarships totaling $25,000 and 1 graduate scholarship total-
ing $5,000.

Nevada
University of Nevada–Reno
Donald W. Reynolds School of Journalism
Reno, NV 89557-0040
James K. Gentry, Dean
B.A.; M.A.
Majors/Sequences: Print, Public Relations, Advertising,
Broadcast Journalism.
Number of scholarships for journalism/mass communication
students: 16, for a total of $35,800.

New Mexico
University of New Mexico
Department of Communication and Journalism
Albuquerque, NM 87131-1171
Everett M. Rogers, Chair
B.A. Journalism; B.A. Communication; M.A.
Communication.
Majors/Sequences: News–Editorial, Broadcast Journalism.
Number of scholarships for journalism/mass communication
students: 5, for a total of $4,950; includes 1 minority scholar-
ship totaling $1,500.

New York
Columbia University
Graduate School of Journalism
New York, NY 10027

Joan Konner, Dean
M.S. Journalism
Major/Sequence: News–Editorial, (graduate).
Number of scholarships for journalism/mass communication
students: 180, for a total of $500,000; includes 24 minority
scholarships totaling $60,000.

New York University
Department of Journalism and Mass Communication
10 Washington Place
New York, NY 10003
Dr. Mitchell Stephens, Chair
B.A. Journalism; M.A. Journalism; M.A. in Journalism and
Caribbean–Latin American Studies; M.A./M.B.A. joint degree
in Journalism and Business; M.A. in Journalism and French;
M.A. in Journalism and Biology; M.A. in Science and Envi-
ronmental Reporting.
Majors/Sequences: News–Editorial, Broadcast News, Maga-
zine, Public Relations, Media Analysis.
Number of scholarships for journalism/mass communication
students: 7, for a total of $12,900; includes 2 minority scholar-
ships totaling $9,300.

Syracuse University
S.I. Newhouse School of Public Communications
Syracuse, NY 13244
David Rubin, Dean
B.S. Public Communications; M.A. Public Communications;
M.S. Public Communications.

North Carolina
University of North Carolina
School of Journalism and Mass Communication
Chapel Hill, NC 27599-3365
Richard R. Cole, Dean
B.A. Journalism; M.A. Journalism
Majors/Sequences: News–Editorial, Advertising, Broadcast
Journalism, Public Relations, Visual Communication,
News–Editorial (graduate).
Number of scholarships for journalism/mass communication
students: 68, for a total of $174,550; includes 5 minority
scholarships totaling $6,000 and 16 graduate scholarships to-
taling $119,300.

Ohio
Bowling Green State University
Department of Journalism
Bowling Green, OH 43403

Raymond Laakaniemi, Chair
B.S. Journalism; M.A. Mass Communication.
Majors/Sequences: News–Editorial, Public Relations, Magazine Journalism, Broadcast Journalism.
Number of scholarships for journalism/mass communication students: 18, for a total of $39,150; includes 2 minority scholarships totaling $400 and 7 graduate scholarships totaling $35,000.

Kent State University
School of Journalism and Mass Communication
Kent, OH 44242-0001
Dr. Timothy D. Smith, Interim Director
B.A. Journalism and Mass Communication; B.S. Journalism and Mass Communication; M.A. Journalism and Mass Communication.
Majors/Sequences: Journalism (newspaper journalism, magazine journalism, and broadcast journalism) Advertising, Public Relations, Photo–Illustration, Photojournalism, Radio–TV Production, Corporate Video, and Media Sales/Management.
Number of scholarships for journalism/mass communication students: 22, for a total of $11,550; includes 1 minority scholarship totaling $500.

Ohio State University
School of Journalism
Columbus, OH 43210-1107
Pamela Shoemaker, Director
B.A. Journalism; M.A. Journalism.
Majors/Sequences: News–Editorial, Broadcast Journalism, Public Relations, Advertising.
Number of scholarships for journalism/mass communication students: 34, for a total of $107,550; includes 1 minority scholarship totaling $750 and 10 graduate scholarships totaling $76,800.

Ohio University
E.W. Scripps School of Journalism
Athens, OH 45701
Dr. Ralph S. Izard, Director
B.S.J. Journalism; M.S.J. Journalism.
Majors/Sequences: News Writing and Editing, Advertising, Magazine, Public Relations, Radio–TV News, Photojournalism.
Number of scholarships for journalism/mass communication students: 250, for a total of $358,015; includes 18 graduate scholarships totaling $123,000.

Oklahoma
Oklahoma State University
School of Journalism and Broadcasting
Stillwater, OK 74078-0195
Dr. Marlan D. Nelson, Director
B.S. Journalism; B.A. Journalism; B.S. Radio–TV; B.A.
Radio–TV; M.S. Mass Communication.
Majors/Sequences: News–Editorial, Broadcast Journalism,
Radio–TV, Advertising, Public Relations.
Number of scholarships for journalism/mass communication
students: 27, for a total of $22,785.

University of Oklahoma
H.H. Herbert School of Journalism and Mass Communication
Norman, OK 73019
Professor David Dary, Director
B.A.J. Journalism; M.A. Journalism.
Majors/sequences: Advertising, News–Communication, Pro-
fessional Writing, Public Relations, Broadcasting.
Number of scholarships for journalism/mass communication
students: 34, for a total of $70,000; includes 3 graduate schol-
arships totaling $2,300.

Oregon
University of Oregon
School of Journalism and Communication
Eugene, OR 97403
Arnold H. Ismach, Dean
B.A. Journalism; B.S. Journalism; M.A. Journalism; M.S.
Journalism.
Majors/Sequences: News–Editorial, Advertising, Electronic
Media, Public Relations, Magazine, Communication Studies.
Number of scholarships for journalism/mass communication
students: 75, for a total of $100,000; includes 15 graduate
scholarships totaling $30,000.

Pennsylvania
Pennsylvania State University
School of Communications
201 Carnegie Bldg.
University Park, PA 16802
Professor Terri Brooks, Dean
B.A. Journalism; B.A. Film/Video; B.A. Advertising; B.A.
Broadcast/Cable; B.A. Media Studies; M.A. Media Studies;
M.A. Telecommunications Studies.
Majors/Sequences: Journalism, Advertising, Broadcast/Cable,

Film and Video, Mass Communications.
Number of scholarships for journalism/mass communication students: 39, for a total of $60,250; includes 4 minority scholarships totaling $6,150 and 1 graduate scholarship totaling $1,000.

Temple University
Department of Journalism
Philadelphia, PA 19122
Dr. David Womack, Chair
B.A. Journalism; M.J. Journalism.
Majors/sequences: News–Editorial, Advertising, Public Relations, Magazines, Photography.
Number of scholarships for journalism/mass communication students: 30, for a total of $108,000; includes 12 graduate scholarships totaling $97,000.

South Carolina
University of South Carolina
College of Journalism and Mass Communications
Columbia, SC 29208
Judy VanSlyke Turk, Dean
B.A. Journalism; M.A. Journalism; M.M.C.
Majors/Sequences: News–Editorial, (newspaper, photojournalism, magazine) Advertising/Public Relations (management, creative advertising) Broadcasting (radio–TV).
Number of scholarships for journalism/mass communication students: 60, for a total of $75,000; includes 1 minority scholarship totaling $6,000.

South Dakota
South Dakota State University
Department of Journalism and Mass Communication
Brookings, SD 57007
Richard W. Lee, Head
B.S. Journalism; B.A. Journalism; M.S. Journalism.
Majors/Sequences: News–Editorial, Broadcast Journalism, Advertising, Science and Technical Writing, Printing Management, Agricultural Journalism, Home Economics Journalism.
Number of scholarships for journalism/mass communication students: 38, for a total of $15,650.

Tennessee
East Tennessee State University
Department of Communication
Johnson City, TN 37614-0667
Dr. Charles Roberts, Chair

B.A. Mass Communications; B.S. Mass Communications.
Majors/Sequences: Journalism, Public Relations, Advertising, Broadcasting.
Number of scholarships for journalism/mass communication students: 5, for a total of $3,550.

Memphis State University
Department of Journalism
Memphis, TN 38152
Dr. Dan Lattimore, Chair
B.A. Journalism; M.A. Journalism.
Majors/Sequences: News–Editorial, (includes magazine, newspaper, and photojournalism), Advertising, Public Relations, Broadcast News.
Number of scholarships for journalism/mass communication students: 14, for a total of $31,000; includes 2 graduate scholarships totaling $3,000.

Middle Tennessee State University
College of Mass Communication
Murfreesboro, TN 37132
Geoffrey Hull, Interim Dean
B.S. Mass Communications; B.S. Recording Industry (Provisional 1993).
Majors/Sequences: Advertising/Public Relations, Journalism, Graphic Communications, Magazine.
Number of scholarships for journalism/mass communication students: 2, for a total of $1,000.

University of Tennessee
College of Communications
Knoxville, TN 37996-0332
Dr. Dwight Teeter, Dean
B.S. Communications; M.S. Communications.
Majors/Sequences: News–Editorial, Broadcast Journalism, Advertising, Public Relations, Professional Program (graduate).
Number of scholarships for journalism/mass communication students: 48, for a total of $161,518; includes 12 minority scholarships totaling $96,144 and 1 graduate scholarship totaling $4,000.

Texas
Texas A&M University
Department of Journalism
College Station, TX 77843-4111
Dr. Charles Self, Head
B.A. Journalism; B.S. Journalism; B.S. Agricultural

Journalism.
Major/Sequence: Journalism.
Number of scholarships for journalism/mass communication students: 12, for a total of $20,800; includes 2 minority scholarships totaling $2,000.

Texas Christian University
Department of Journalism
P.O. Box 32930
Fort Worth, TX 76129
Dr. Anantha S. Babbili, Chair
B.A. Journalism; B.S. Journalism; M.S. Media Studies.
Majors/Sequences: News–Editorial, Broadcast Journalism, Advertising/Public Relations, Teaching Certification.
Number of scholarships for journalism/mass communication students: 16, for a total of $56,700; includes 8 graduate scholarships totaling $50,000.

Texas Tech University
School of Mass Communications
Lubbock, TX 79409-3082
Dr. Roger Saathoff, Director
B.A. Journalism; B.A. Advertising; B.A. Public Relations; B.A. Telecommunications; B.A. Photocommunications; M.A. Mass Communications.
Majors/Sequences: News–Editorial, Advertising, Telecommunications, Public Relations, Photocommunications, Broadcast Journalism, Corporate Telecommunications, Professional Program (graduate).
Number of scholarships for journalism/mass communication students: 55, for a total of $33,800; includes 1 minority scholarship totaling $400 and 5 graduate scholarships totaling $18,600.

University of North Texas
Department of Journalism
Denton, TX 76203-5278
Dr. Richard Wells, Chair
B.A. Journalism; B.S. Journalism; M.A. Journalism; M.J. Journalism.
Majors/Sequences: News–Editorial, Advertising, Public Relations, Business Journalism, Photojournalism, Teaching Journalism, Broadcast News.
Number of scholarships for journalism/mass communication students: 12, for a total of $22,000; includes 5 minority scholarships totaling $1,200 and 2 graduate scholarships totaling $12,500.

University of Texas
Department of Journalism
Austin, TX 78712
Russell G. Todd, Chair
B.J. Journalism; M.A. Journalism.
Number of scholarships for journalism/mass communication
students: 39, for a total of $90,500; includes 2 minority schol-
arships totaling $10,000 and 5 graduate scholarships totaling
$32,500.

Utah

Brigham Young University
Department of Communications
Room E509
Harris Fine Arts Center
Provo, UT 84602
Dr. David P. Forsyth, Chair
B.A. Communications; M.A. Communications.
Major/Sequence: Journalism (print, advertising, public rela-
tions, radio–TV news, broadcast production).
Number of scholarships for journalism/mass communication
students: 20, for a total of $62,520, includes 5 minority schol-
arships totaling $25,000 and 10 graduate scholarships totaling
$23,071, and 2 Donald W. Reynolds undergraduate scholar-
ships totaling $5,000.

University of Utah
Department of Communication LCB 204
Salt Lake City, UT 84112
Dr. James A. Anderson, Chair
B.S. Mass Communication; B.A. Mass Communication; M.S.
Mass Communication; M.A. Mass Communication.
Majors/Sequences: News–Editorial, Public Relations, Broad-
cast News and Production, Photojournalism, Telecommunica-
tion and Film, Integrated Marketing Communication
(post-baccalaureate certificate).
Number of scholarships for journalism/mass communication
students: 28, for a total of $130,750; includes 12 graduate
scholarships totaling $104,000.

Virginia

Virginia Commonwealth University
School of Mass Communications
Richmond, VA 23284
Thomas Donohue, Director
B.S. Mass Communications; M.S. Mass Communications.

Majors/Sequences: News–Editorial, Broadcasting/Electronic Media, Advertising/Public Relations.
Number of scholarships for journalism/mass communication students: 16, for a total of $64,450; includes 6 graduate scholarships totaling $60,000.

Washington and Lee University
Department of Journalism and Mass Communications
Lexington, VA 24450
Professor Hampden H. Smith, III, Head
B.A.
Majors/Sequences: News–Editorial, Radio–TV News, Communications.
Number of scholarships for journalism/mass communication students: 8, for a total of $10,000.

Washington
University of Washington
School of Communications
DS-40
Seattle, WA 98195
Dr. Edward P. Bassett
B.A. Arts and Sciences; M.A. Arts and Sciences; M.C. Communications.
Majors/Sequences: Editorial Journalism, Advertising, Broadcast Journalism, Public Relations, Communication (graduate only), Media Studies (evening division only).
Number of scholarships for journalism/mass communication students: 20, for a total of $68,000; includes 10 minority scholarships totaling $13,000 and 5 graduate scholarships totaling $25,000.

West Virginia
Marshall University
W. Page Pitt School of Journalism and Mass Communications
Huntington, WV 25755
Dr. Harold Shaver, Director
B.A. Journalism; M.A.J. Journalism.
Majors/Sequences: News–Editorial, Advertising, Public Relations, Broadcast Journalism, Magazine, Journalism Education, Broadcasting.
Number of scholarships for journalism/mass communication students: 49, for a total of $40,665; includes 8 graduate scholarships totaling $24,000.

West Virginia University
Perley Isaac Reed School of Journalism
Morgantown, WV 26506-6010

Dr. Emery L. Sasser, Dean
B.S.J. Journalism; M.S.J. Journalism.
Majors/Sequences: News–Editorial, Advertising, Public Relations, Broadcast News.
Number of scholarships for journalism/mass communication students: 27, for a total of $57,500; includes 4 minority scholarships totaling $2,000 and 5 graduate scholarships totaling $27,500.

Wisconsin
Marquette University
College of Communication, Journalism, and Performing Arts
Milwaukee, WI 53233
Dr. Sharon M. Murphy, Dean
B.A. Advertising; B.A. Broadcast and Electronic Communication; B.A. Public Relations; B.A.J. Journalism; M.A. Advertising; M.A. Broadcast and Electronic Communication; M.A. Journalism; M.A. Public Relations.
Majors/Sequences: News–Editorial, Magazine, Photojournalism.
Number of scholarships for journalism/mass communication students: 47, for a total of $301,650; includes 2 minority scholarships totaling $5,750 and 27 graduate scholarships totaling $210,500.

University of Wisconsin–Eau Claire
Department of Journalism
Eau Claire, WI 54702-4004
W. Robert Sampson, Acting Administrator
B.A. Journalism; B.S. Journalism.
Majors/Sequences: News–Editorial, Advertising, Radio–TV, Secondary School.
Number of scholarships for journalism/mass communication students: 10, for a total of $2,800.

University of Wisconsin–Madison
Department of Agricultural Journalism
Madison, WI 53706
Marion Brown, Chair
B.S. Agricultural Journalism; M.S. Agricultural Journalism; B.S. Family and Consumer Journalism; M.S. Family and Consumer Journalism (Provisional 1993).
Majors/Sequences: News–Editorial, Advertising, Broadcast News, Public Relations, Mass Communications.
Number of scholarships for journalism/mass communication students: 70, for a total of $30,500; includes 9 minority scholarships totaling $4,450.

University of Wisconsin–Oshkosh
Department of Journalism
Oshkosh, WI 54901-8696
Gene Hintz, Chair
B.A. Journalism; B.S. Journalism
Majors/Sequences: News–Editorial, Advertising–Public
Relations.
Number of scholarships for journalism/mass communication
students: 5, for a total of $2,000.

University of Wisconsin
Department of Journalism
River Falls, WI 54022
J. Michael Norman, Chair
B.A. Journalism; B.S. Journalism.
Majors/Sequences: News–Editorial, Broadcast Journalism,
Agricultural Journalism, Secondary Journalism Education.
Number of scholarships for journalism/mass communication
students: 8, for a total of $2,100.

Canada
Carleton University
School of Journalism and Communication
Ottawa, Ontario K1S 5B6
Professor P. Johansen, Director
Majors/Sequences: Print, Radio–TV, Radio Documentary,
Film Documentary, International Affairs, Political Affairs.
Number of scholarships for journalism/mass communication
students: 29, for a total of $25,425; includes 16 graduate
scholarships totaling $14,700.

Concordia University
Department of Journalism
7141 Sherbrooke St. W.
Montreal, Quebec H4B-1R6
Lindsay Crysler, Director of Journalism
Majors/Sequences: News–Editorial, Specialization in Commu-
nication and Journalism, Broadcast Journalism.
Number of scholarships for journalism/mass communication
students: 6, for a total of $7,000; includes 2 graduate scholar-
ships totaling $4,000.

Ryerson Polytechnic Institute
School of Journalism
350 Victoria Street
Toronto, Ontario M5B 2K3
John Miller, Chair

Majors/Sequences: Print, Broadcast Journalism, Magazine.
Number of scholarships for journalism/mass communication
students: 35, for a total of $30,000; includes 12 graduate
scholarships totaling $9,000.

University of King's College
School of Journalism
Halifax, Nova Scotia B3H2A1
Professor Michael Cobden, Director
Majors/Sequences: News–Editorial, Broadcast News.

University of Regina
School of Journalism and Mass Communications
Education Building, Room 133
Regina, Saskatchewan S4S 0A2
Sat Kumar, Director
Majors/Sequences: News–Editorial, Magazine, Broadcasting,
Photography.
Number of scholarships for journalism/mass communication
students: 12, for a total of $12,500.

University of Western Ontario
Graduate School of Journalism
London, Ontario N6A 5B7
Peter Desbarats, Dean
Majors/Sequences: Print, Broadcasting, Journalism.
Number of scholarships for journalism/mass communication
students: 3, for a total of $6,000; includes 1 minority scholar-
ship totaling $2,000 and 2 graduate scholarships totaling
$4,000.

In addition to these institutions, there are many colleges and universities
all over North America that offer journalism programs or liberal arts programs with journalism classes. Many junior colleges also offer journalism,
technical and creative writing, and mass communication opportunities. Upon
completing a two-year sequence, newspaper trade groups and others encourage students to transfer to a four-year college to finish their studies and earn
a bachelor's degree. There are also special programs available, such as the
Unversity of Chicago's Publishing Program, Radcliffe's Publishing Course,
and Stanford's Professional Publishing Course.

Seek out the schools in your desired location and make a careful evaluation based on the factors previously discussed and any others that are important to *you*. Visit those places that are feasible and interest you most, talk to
faculty and students, sit in on some classes, become enmeshed in the school
and its surroundings, and you'll get a feel for what is right for *you*.

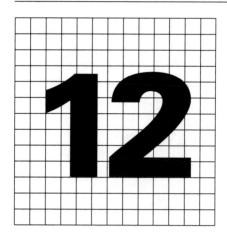

WORK EXPERIENCE AND EXTRACURRICULAR ACTIVITIES

For several days after my first book was published I carried it about in my pocket, and took surreptitious peeps at it to make sure the ink had not faded.

—James M. Barrie

Mr. Rogers was the Reverend Fred Rogers before he made his home in everyone's favorite public television neighborhood. David Brinkley started out as "something beneath a reporter" at a Wilmington, North Carolina newspaper. Barry Manilow is quoted as saying, "I got my start in the CBS mailroom," the site that launched a number of careers, it is said, including Walter Cronkite's. The message is clear: Everyone starts somewhere and works up from there.

MAKE THE MOST OF YOUR HIGH SCHOOL YEARS

Preparing yourself for a career in journalism may easily begin at the junior high or high school level. Following a college preparatory course of study and earning excellent grades are important, but you can engage in a host of other activities that will give you experience and enhance your journalism career path opportunities. Here are some of those possibilities:

1. *Journals.* Keep a journal and write in it every day. This gives you practice in writing, analyzing, and putting thoughts together. It also makes you aware and observant of what is going on around you. These are all valuable skills for journalists.

2. *Read, read, read.* Read newspapers, news magazines, and magazines on a regular basis. This will keep you up-to-date on current events. Read biographies of successful journalists. How did they become famous? What can you glean from their lives that you can implement in your own? Read everything else you can get your hands on—the more you read, the more you'll know.

3. *Write, write, write.* Innate talent is a wonderful gift but regardless of the amount you possess, the most important endeavor you can engage in is practicing, experimenting, and honing your craft.

4. *Extracurricular clubs or classes.* Enroll in any journalism, speech, photography, or drama classes or clubs your school has to offer.

5. *Journalistic or photographic organizations.* Join any organizations that allow high school students to join their ranks.

6. *Public speaking.* Take part in debate clubs, student council organizations, or any other school government associations. This will help you acquire public speaking skills and make you more relaxed with speaking in public.

7. *Professional contacts.* Talk to teachers who have personal knowledge of this field or who may refer you to others who do. Ask questions about their careers, what their responsibilities are, and what advice they might be willing to provide for you.

8. *School radio or television.* If your school has any connection with a radio or television station, participate in some way.

9. *School newspaper, yearbook, or other publication.* Volunteer to help with any publications your school offers. This is an ideal way to gain valuable skills and experience that prospective employers value highly. Learn everything you can about reporting, editing, layout, and advertising.

10. *Published work.* Submit your work for publication. Find sources to send your work to in the most current editions of *Writer's Market, The Writer's Handbook,* or *Literary Market Place* (among others). Local newspapers and newsletters are always good possibilities, too.

11. *Workshops, seminars, and other educational meetings.* A wide variety of activities are planned each year by many organizations. The Dow Jones Newspaper Fund, for example, offers a variety of high school journalism workshops specifically geared for minority students. Check with your career counselor, English or journalism teacher, or local librarian for details.

12. *Local television or radio station.* If you are lucky enough to have a television or radio station nearby, hang around as much as possible. Observe and absorb what you observe. Offer to lend a hand whenever possible.

13. *Community or religious newsletters.* Volunteering to work on community or religious newsletters in any capacity gives you an insight into how they are created, written, and put together. All of this is excellent experience.

14. Local newspaper. Familiarize yourself with the newspapers in your area. Go to the library and study *Editor and Publisher Yearbook* or the *Gale Directory of Publications.* Then contact your local newspaper to volunteer your services as a part-time or summer reporter. Pay is secondary to the experience you will gain.

15. *College search.* Allow more than ample time to thoroughly investigate and evaluate all possibilities before making a final college choice.

MAKE THE MOST OF YOUR COLLEGE YEARS

All of the suggestions offered to high school students also apply to those at the college level. In addition, college students have some other options, such as the following (a breakdown of undergraduate activities is shown in Figure 12.1):

1. *Internships.* Internships provide you with invaluable on-the-job experience and offer a realistic first-hand view of at least one area of the world of publishing. Whether they offer any remuneration is irrelevant; they will pay off in the long run. Internships add depth to your resume and provide a network for job opportunities. Indeed, interns are often hired as regular employees.

    The more internships you have, the better. Look into the many programs that are available (for example, the American Society of Magazine Editors internship) and do it early. Consult one of the guides listed at the end of this chapter for more complete information on this topic.

2. *On-campus communication programs.* In addition to campus newspapers, many larger campuses have radio stations and possibly even television stations and film laboratories. Some community colleges produce programs for cable channels. If this is the case at your school, take advantage of these opportunities.

3. *Professional organizations.* Join organizations such as the Society for Collegiate Journalists, Sigma Delta Chi, and Associated Collegiate Press. Become active in any way possible.

RESOURCES FOR INFORMATION ABOUT INTERNSHIPS

Internships
c/o Peterson's
202 Carnegie Center, P.O. Box 2123
Princeton, New Jersey 08543-2123

Internships, Volume 2
The Career Press Inc.
P.O. Box 34
Hawthorne, New Jersey 07507

The Journalist's Road to Success: A Career and Scholarship Guide
Dow Jones Newspaper Fund
P.O. Box 300
Princeton, New Jersey 08543-0300

Figure 12.1 Campus Activities of Bachelor's Degree recipients (in Percentages)

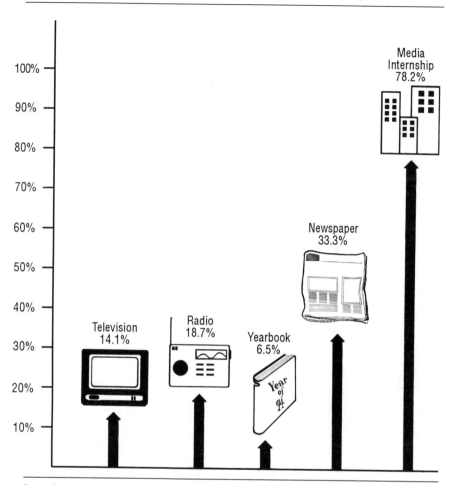

Source: Summary results from the 1992 Annual Graduate Survey by Lee B. Becker and Gerald M. Kosicki, School of Journalism, The Ohio State University. Project sponsors for 1992 were The Dow Jones Newspaper Fund, The National Association of Broadcasters, The Association for Education in Journalism and Mass Communication, The Council of Affiliates of the Association for Education in Journalism and Mass Communication, The Association of Schools of Journalism and Mass Communication, and The School of Journalism at The Ohio State University.

The National Directory of Internships
The National Society for Internships and
Experiential Education
3509 Haworth Drive, Suite 207
Raleigh, North Carolina 27609

Scholarships, Fellowships, and Loans
Gale Research Inc.
835 Penobscot Building
Detroit, Michigan 48226-4094

The Student Guide to Mass Media Internships
School of Journalism and Mass Communication
University of Colorado
Boulder, Colorado 80309

These resources should be available in your school library, local library, or career guidance office.

DESIRABLE SKILLS, ABILITIES, AND ATTRIBUTES

He that will write well in any tongue must follow this counsel of Aristotle: to speak as the common people do, to think as wise men do.

—Roger Ascham

When defining characteristics needed by journalists, experts agree that writers must be capable of producing clear, clean copy. What does that mean? First and foremost, it means that the writing must be easy to understand. What makes a piece of writing easy to understand? For one thing, words have been used correctly and put together in a meaningful way. Readers don't have to reread passages over and over to figure out what the author is trying to say. Sentence structure is correct, making the writer's intent clear. There are no extraneous words or jargon; every word has a purpose. Subjects and pronouns are clearly identified so you don't have to guess who is saying what to whom. Words of three or more syllables are used only when appropriate, not strictly for effect. Grammar, punctuation, and vocabulary are correct; this pleases not only English teachers, but all readers, who are confused when there are errors.

Writers should realize that even computer spellchecks cannot pick up all spelling errors. After all, a computer won't single out a word as an error if what you've typed is a legitimate word. Computers don't understand that you meant an entirely different word with a different meaning.

Those of you who are lacking a strong foundation in these areas should buy (and study) one of the good books on the market, such as *The Elements of Grammar* by Margaret Shertzer (Collier Books, Macmillan Publishing Company, New York, 1986) or *Barron's Essentials of English,* 4th edition by Vincent F. Hopper, Cedric Gale, and Ronald C. Foote, (revised by Benjamin W. Griffith, New York, 1990). Even if you feel confident about your skills, purchase one of these books to keep for reference. Everyone feels the need for verification occasionally.

There are many other skills that writers work a lifetime to perfect: developing ideas into stories or books and creating strong beginnings, satisfying endings, convincing characterization, and well-crafted plotting. Writers must also concentrate on formulating a pleasing style, smooth transitions, effective dialogue, crisp description, and a consistent viewpoint (from whose perspective is the story told).

RESEARCH

Virtually every type of effective writing, both fiction and nonfiction is based on research. All research involves a process of investigation not unlike that conducted by the famous Sherlock Holmes. This famous detective located and studied clues that provided information leading to other clues and so on until he solved the case. Researchers must search for sources (clues) to provide them with information leading to other sources and eventually enough information to write the article or book. Once they are able to put the clues (all the information they've uncovered) together they've solved the case.

All fiction writers know that even though they are creating a story and a cast of characters out of their imaginations, the final product will only work if it is founded in truth. For instance, a mystery writer who murders a character with cyanide poisoning better know all of the following: where and if cyanide is easily obtainable, how long it takes before it works, what effect it has on the body, what constitutes a lethal dose, and what traces, if any, it leaves. Readers demand that writers, even in fictional works, understand the tools they use. Have you ever read something that did not jibe with what you already knew to be true? Did you feel as if the author didn't do his or her homework? These things bother us and we may feel that this writer is not worthy of our time, attention, or book dollars.

INTERVIEWING

With few exceptions, all writers see interviewing as an integral part of their research. Newspaper journalists, feature writers, article and book authors, technical writers, fiction and nonfiction specialists, business writers, and most other types of writers use interviews to provide background information, expert testimony, direct quotes from those involved with the topic, substantiation of their conclusions, and, possibly most important, a humanization of their topic.

When you approach interview subjects, you should identify yourself and your credentials, discuss the nature of your project, and identify for whom you are working. Then explain why you would like to interview them, what this would entail, and when you would need to accomplish this. Surprisingly, most individuals are happy to cooperate with you. Once you receive a positive answer, your work begins. Research everything possible about that individual and your topic. From this information, you will draft your list of tentative questions.

If you are doing a personal interview, bring your list of well-conceived questions, pens, paper, notebooks, tape recorder, several blank tapes, and spare batteries. But before you do anything, concentrate on putting your subject at ease. This may be accomplished by making small talk or initiating conversation on a nonthreatening issue, such as the subject's hobby or interest. When you feel he or she is relaxed, begin with general questions that will give you a feel for this individual's personality. Then proceed to other questions that are more specific and perhaps more meaningful. Be prepared to guide the interview, but also allow it to take its natural course. If the subject really strays from your original focus, ask a question to get him or her to zero in on the issue at hand.

Here are some other useful tips:

1. Practice your interviewing skills with friends and family beforehand. Having experience will make you feel more relaxed and that will be passed along to your subject. The more comfortable your subject feels, the better the interview will turn out.

2. Select a location with few distractions.

3. Dress appropriately. If you are meeting at a business office, wear a professional outfit. If the interview is held at the subject's home or a neighborhood restaurant, casual attire is permissible.

4. Be sure you have all basic information correct: the subject's full name (and its correct spelling), address, telephone number, company name, title, and any other pertinent details.

5. Don't display any antagonism, even if what the person endorses is contrary to what you believe. This is not a forum for you to debate.

6. *Listen carefully* both to what is being said and what is not being said. Read between the lines. If the interview is done in person, observe body language.

7. Show empathy.

8. Nod your head or make some sound that shows you are listening and "with" the person who is talking. No one likes to talk indefinitely with no sign of someone listening.

9. Save your penetrating questions for the end of the interview. Your subject will more likely be relaxed by then and in a mood to answer your questions.

10. If taking notes, date and label the entries. Record only what is relevant, not every word uttered by your subject. Sometimes this is difficult, especially when you are not sure whether the information is germane until later. Jot things down as quickly as possible, devising some method of speed writing. If you will be using the same word or name several times, use a letter or number for identification. Listen for key ideas or phrases, pick up on speech inflections that indicate extra emphasis. Have your thoughts on what you are writing, not on what the subject is saying or

your next question. If you are frantically trying to keep up, ask him or her to pause for a moment. Type up your notes into some intelligible form as soon as possible.

11. If you record your interview, make *sure* your tape recorder is operative. Some experts advise against this because of the possibility of malfunction. My recommendation is to bring one along, but to also take copious notes so you have a backup. I'd also advise that you test the tape immediately after the interview so that if there is a problem you can sit down at your computer right away and record everything before your memory fades.

    Though it's true that transcribing tapes eats up a great deal of time, you get the entire interview verbatim. If someone discusses something with you and asks that it be "off the record," you are honor bound to exclude it from the written interview.

12. If the interview is conducted by phone, obtain permission before taping, use a speakerphone on the loudest setting, jot down impressions as you go along, and transcribe the tape and your notes as soon as possible.

13. Always be sure to thank the subject for his or her information and time. If an advance copy of your final written piece is requested, let the subject know when he or she might receive it and when the actual magazine or book will be published.

Half of the skill in effective interviewing is technical, and the other half is a combination of instinct and skilled experience, being able to ask an intriguing or revealing question at the right moment or evoking a response that puts the subject in a new light, explains the topic more clearly, or facilitates the reader's ability to relate to it on a deeper level.

ORGANIZATION

Once interviewing and other kinds of research and note taking are accomplished, journalists look to their organizational skills. After all, what do you do with the mountains of information you have collected. Do you include all of it? How do you know when you have enough information? How do you organize it? How do you decide what to leave out? In what order do you present it?

These questions can only be answered by examining your audience and the prescribed length and purpose of your piece. Once you have clearly established for whom you are writing and what you hope the piece will accomplish, measure all information against these standards. What furthers or solidifies your purpose should be included and what is not relevant, should not be.

In order to organize the article, you may link interview ideas that flow naturally from one to the other, but you should never misrepresent what has been said. Changing a few words to provide clarity is permissible, but changing a person's intent is *never acceptable and is quite unethical.*

OTHER DESIRABLE QUALITIES

Other personal qualities that management-level personnel mention as desirable for journalists are the ability to take responsibility, intellectual curiosity, enthusiasm, creativity, a broad range of knowledge, an affinity for people, motivation, and persistence. Employers also seek voracious readers, excellent communicators (both oral and written), good listeners, outgoing personalities, and those with an understanding of human psychology. Candidates must be adaptable, prepared, accurate, pleasant, sincere, tactful, self-confident, assertive, and imaginative. And if that's not enough, employers also cite physical and mental stamina, energy, dedication, courage, initiative, poise, a sense of humor, good judgment, and the ability to take criticism.

Broadcast journalists usually need some element of "show business" appeal, such as physical attractiveness, a neat appearance, a pleasant personality, and an appealing voice. It is also important to have an aggressive approach, social awareness, a competitive spirit, and an interest in and knowledge of current events and the operation of government at all levels.

Those employed by newspapers, magazines, government agencies, businesses, or other associations must be able to work effectively on their own and as members of groups. They must display problem-solving abilities; phone, computer, and typing proficiency; tenacity; business savvy; a good memory; poise; and self-discipline. All journalists must be able to work quickly and accurately under the pressure of deadlines. Desired are those who are goal oriented, have a belief in their own abilities, and have a sincere love for the English language. Journalists who seek promotions to management-level positions must have administrative capabilities, a desire and competency for increased authority, skill in delegating, and the ability to complete projects by interacting with personnel from a number of other departments.

Part Four
Beginning Your Career

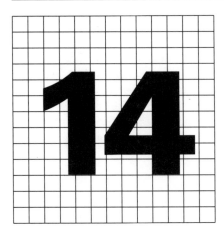

JOB STRATEGIES

Far and away the best prize that life offers is the chance to work hard at work worth doing.

—Theodore Roosevelt

The field of journalism offers many diverse career possibilities; all of which offer you the chance, as Roosevelt says, to work hard at work worth doing. Sometimes securing a position may also involve hard work. But work worth doing is something you view with passion and love. That's where your job search should begin.

GOAL SETTING

Setting goals is important at all stages of life and in all phases of a career, but particularly as you begin your job search. Although it is important to be flexible, you must focus on the type of work you want to do and the setting you prefer: Have something specific in mind. For example, "I want to be a general reporter working for a local newspaper." Once you do this, you can focus your energies in a very specific direction.

You also need to be realistic. If you do not have much experience, you should expect to begin with an entry-level position. As a rule, this will mean starting at a small publication or station or in a rural area. Generally you need several years of experience before being considered by larger city newspapers, national magazines, or large television or radio stations. Often it is in your best interests to accept a secretarial or office assistant's job to get your foot in the door. If your job search is not going well and you can afford it, volunteer to work for a week without pay. Then show everyone how indispensable you are and wait for an offer.

LOOKING FOR OPPORTUNITIES

There are many sources to explore in your job search. The following sections describe the most commonly used resources.

Networking   This is the way the majority of people find jobs. You must make a concerted effort to let people know that you are looking for a position. Talk to friends and acquaintances; go to club meetings and association workshops. Volunteer to help with an event. Converse with people you deal with in everyday life: cleaners, bank tellers, personal accountants, anyone you can think of. Of course, you may not hear about an opening directly, but one person may give you the name of another person to contact and so on and so on. It may become a treasure hunt where one place leads you to the next until you find the "gems" and locate a possible position.

College or University Placement Services   School placement services may be very helpful in locating positions for you and guiding you in your job search. Work closely with these human resource professionals who can give you a lot of worthwhile advice. Some schools have job fairs and/or contact with employers who come to the school to recruit students.

Newspaper Advertisements   This is still a popular form of securing jobs. You should obtain copies of local local and regional newspapers and read the ads all the way through. In the world of journalism, jobs may be listed under headings you wouldn't think of. Also, even though some ads may be seeking people in other areas, they may reveal names of companies you were not aware of. Virtually every company could benefit from the services of a journalist in a number of capacities, so check them out.

Professional Organizations   These groups often advertise for help in their newsletters and journals. Some have specialized services, such as The International Association of Business Communicators (IABC), who maintains a "Jobline" job bank service that gives callers up-to-date information on job openings. Other examples are the Public Relations Society of America's (PRSA) *Journal,* which includes advertisements for communication jobs, and The National Association of Science Writers' newsletter, *Science Writers,* which lists openings for science writers.

Trade Publications   A number of publications, such as *Editor and Publisher* and *The Quill,* include job openings and information.

Private Employers   Approach companies directly. A high percentage of jobs are never listed anywhere, and many people secure positions by calling or sending letters to specific companies. Rather than sending out mass mailings, you are better off targeting your efforts to particular companies that you have researched.

Always obtain the name of a specific person to direct your letters to and, if possible, secure a referral name. Send your resume and a targeted cover letter. You may also choose to include clips or addenda.

Lists of possible employers may be created by using reference books available at most libraries. For those seeking work on newspapers, for example, *Editor and Publisher International Year Book* lists names and addresses of papers all over the world. Write or visit the editors of newspapers that interest you. *The Gale Directory of Publications and Broadcast Media* is an excellent resource for newspapers, magazines, radio stations, television stations, and cable systems.

There are many other reference books of this nature. Ask your local librarian for assistance.

Federal, State, and Local Government Personnel Offices

These agencies list a wide range of possibilities for all types of fields. Look up listings for "Government" in your local phone book.

The U.S. Department of Labor offers the following information on organizations for specific groups:

Disabled
President's Committee on Employment of
People with Disabilities
1331 F St. NW, 3rd Floor
Washington, DC 20004

Minorities
National Urban League
Employment Department
500 E. 62nd St.
New York, NY 10021

Older Workers
American Association of Retired Persons
Worker Equity
601 E St. NW, Floor A5
Washington, DC 20049

Veterans
Contact the nearest regional office of the
Veterans Administration.

Women
Catalyst
250 Park Avenue South, 5th Floor
New York, NY 10003

(Ask for the free referral pamphlet called *Career Development Resources.*)

**Employment Agencies
and Career Consultants**   You may be responsible for fees but it may be worth it.

PREPARING FOR A JOB SEARCH

Getting ready for a job search is like getting ready to do battle; you must arm yourself with all the best weapons available to you and plan the best possible plan of attack. The best weapons available to you include a well-designed resume, a well-conceived cover letter, a well-selected portfolio, writing addenda (to list your writing credits), and an audition tape, clips, or other samples of your work. These materials provide a base from which you will market yourself.

Resumes   A resume should include significant information that would make an employer want to hire you above all others. Standing as a summary of your experience, skills and abilities, strengths, and education, its importance cannot be underestimated. A job search involves a number of customary steps; if your resume is lacking, you will never advance to the steps that lead to a job offer. Thus, much thought must go into how to best present the pertinent information.

Experts agree the best approach is to keep it focused and as brief as possible. Complete sentences are not necessary; phrases are acceptable. No one has much time these days, and a lengthy resume may simply go unread. Keep yours to a maximum of two pages; one is even better. Don't list everything you ever did in your life; highlight important skills and accomplishments.

As a candidate in the general field of communications, your resume will be scrutinized especially carefully. Thus, the writing, organization, and composition of your resume must be of a very high caliber. Any errors will undoubtedly eliminate your chances for placement with an organization. Knowing that should make you realize just how important this is.

One popular type of resume, the *chronological resume* (illustrated in Figure 14.1), includes the following elements:

1. *Heading.* Provide a heading at the top of the page that includes your name, home address, and phone number(s). If it is possible for you to receive calls at your present work location, include that number. If not, consider investing in an answering machine that will take messages during business hours when you are away and prospective employers are most apt to call. Most machines have features that allow you to retrieve messages while you are out, so you will be able to return these important calls at lunchtime or on breaks.

2. *Job objective.* Most experts say that you should next indicate a job objective on your resume. Usually one sentence long, the job objective pinpoints your employment goal. An example would be: "To se-

cure an editorial position with a local newspaper." Some people add a reference to their skills, such as the following: "A technical writing position where I may utilize my science and math background." Some experts advise you to include your objective in your cover letter. You may use either method.

3. *Work experience.* This will be the main part of your resume, where your prospective employers will focus to determine whether or not you have the right qualifications for the job. So here is where you must show your expertise by emphasizing your accomplishments. Do this by using action verbs. Passive words do not have the same impact. Tell how you researched, implemented, evaluated, developed, improved, produced, administered, published, negotiated, and communicated. These words describe you as someone who isn't afraid to take responsibility, seize opportunities, and work hard. These phrases show results.

   Work experience is usually listed in reverse chronological order beginning with your most recent position and working back. Entries should be complete, listing the job title, dates of employment, employer, and location.

4. *Education.* Next to work experience, education is most important, and in fact, those with less experience will be judged even more on their educational backgrounds. Include the schools you've attended, the degrees you've earned, your field of concentration, and relevant extracurricular activities (Yearbook Editor, for example). You may also include any journalism seminars and workshops you've attended.

5. *Professional associations.* Professional affiliations or associations in journalism will indicate your interest in the field.

6. *Awards and honors.* Include any awards and honors you've received, such as the following: Abraham Lincoln State Scholarship 1991, or Dean's List, 1992.

7. *Special skills.* Additional abilities, such as computer and foreign language competencies, may also be desirable attributes to employers.

8. *References.* Make a notation that references are available upon request or include the actual references. The Dow Jones Newspaper Fund reports that newspaper editors prefer to see references as a part of the resume.

For those who are recent graduates, internships, part-time positions, other work experience, and educational background will play an important role in being hired.

Those who have been out of school for a number of years and have held several positions may find another style of resume, the functional resume, preferable. Here you offer your achievements first to stress what you have accomplished already, making what you did more important than where you were working at the time. An example of a functional resume is shown in Figure 14.2.

Figure 14.1 Sample Chronological Resume

WENDY WIMMER

45330 Santa Monica Blvd.
Los Angeles, CA 90088
(213) 555-8393 (Day)
(213) 555-3839 (Evening)

OBJECTIVE:	Senior Copywriter for a publishing company.
EMPLOYMENT EXPERIENCE:	Winterpark Publishing, Inc., Pasadena, CA Staff Copywriter, 1991–present Researched and wrote book proposals, including sales letters, synopsis, and sample chapters. Created advertising copy for company's book catalogs. Composed captions for illustrations and side bars. Handled layout and paste-up. Edited and rewrote manuscripts in preparation for publication.
	Wendy Wimmer, Inc., Los Angeles, CA Freelance Writer, 1987–1991 Edited five technical manuals on computer software. Scripted four industrial films for various food service companies. Developed two book ideas and drafted sales proposals for book pacaking company. Wrote several articles published in national magazines. Composed copy for department store catalog.
EDUCATION:	University of California–Los Angeles, Los Angeles, CA B.A. in English, 1987
HONORS:	Phi Beta Kappa, 1987 Dean's List, 1986, 1987 Robert D. Mayo Writing Competition, Second Prize, 1986 Writing Club, President, 1987

References available upon request

Figure 14.2 Sample Functional Resume

ROSEMARY DEBORAH PARKER

5509 E. George St. #442
Columbia, SC 29263
(803) 555-2893

CAREER OBJECTIVE: Magazine editor

SKILLS AND ACCOMPLISHMENTS:

- Evaluated submitted manuscripts for a monthly magazine.
- Handled copy editing and rewriting of manuscripts.
- Worked with artists and designers on layout aspects.
- Supervised the publication of an anthology of poetry.
- Served as proofreader for feature articles.
- Handled copy editing duties for local newspaper.
- Reported on events of local interest.
- Represented employer at several publishing conferences.

EMPLOYMENT HISTORY:

Carolina Woman, Columbia, SC
   Assistant Editor, 1987–present

Raleigh Gazette, Raleigh, NC
   Copy editor/reporter, 1984–1987

EDUCATION:
   Columbia University, Columbia, SC
   B.A. in Journalism, 1984
   Minor in English

HONORS:
   Summa Cum Laude
   Journalism Award, 1983
   Henry Moffatt Scholarship recipient, 1981–1984

MEMBERSHIPS:

   Southern Writers Association
   American Association of Magazine Publishers

References available upon request

Figure 14.3 Resume Combining Chronological and Functional Elements

SAMUEL TRAVIS SHAVERS

15 E. Greenview St. #333
Richmond, VA 18978
(804) 555-3903

EDUCATION

University of Virginia, Richmond, VA
B.A. in Journalism, 1994

Hawkins Journalism Scholarship, 1991, 1992
Interned with WRCH-TV, senior year
Vice president, senior class

WRITING EXPERIENCE

- Served as Senior Editor of campus newspaper: selected articles, approved editorials, edited and wrote copy, supervised seven writers.
- Assisted in the editing of literary magazine Flight: proofread and edited copy.
- Researched stories for local television news station.
- Wrote a weekly column for campus newspaper: actively pursued investigative reporting, handled both campus and local community events.
- Created design and layout for 1992 Freshman Handbook; assisted with typesetting and offset printing of handbook.

WORK HISTORY

University of Virginia, Richmond, VA
Senior Editor, Campus Newspaper, 1993–1994
Editor, Flight, 1993
Designer, Freshman Handbook, 1992
Writer, Campus Newspaper, 1991–1992

WRCH-TV, Richmond, VA
Intern, 1993

MEMBERSHIPS

Association of College Journalists, 1993–1994
Virginia Literary Society, 1992

REFERENCES

Available upon request

There is a third type of resume that combines both the chronological and functional formats, as in Figure 14.3. Deciding which kind of resume to use should rest on whatever method best highlights your talents, experience, and abilities.

Some experts advise you to revise and adjust your resume to specifically target particular positions or companies. Resumes to magazine editors, for instance, should emphasize feature and article writing experience, whereas a resume to a local business should emphasize your experience in writing press releases, brochures, and sales letters. If you have a variety of experience performing a number of tasks, you may want to do this.

To make the resume look appealing leave one- to one-and-one-half-inch margins on all sides. Keep ample space between sections; two or three lines are adequate. Be consistent using capitals or boldface type. There is no right or wrong style; simply be consistent. Resumes should be printed on good quality white or off-white paper using type that is easy to read. Proofread your resume a number of times to make sure there are no grammar, spelling, punctuation, or capitalization errors. Have someone else read it too. A new pair of eyes will often pick up something you've missed.

There are some things you should definitely leave out: personal information, such as marital status; social club affiliation; salary history or requirements; jobs that have nothing to do with this field; repetitious statements; and *anything that could possibly show you in a negative light.* Last, but certainly not least, if you have a computer, keep your resume on a disk and adapt or update it as needed.

Cover Letters

A cover letter is a document that sells the recipient on reading the resume. It should be directed to a specific person whose name and spelling you have verified. Cover letters should be tailored to each specific company or job opening. Don't use a form letter here, although some of the information, including the job you are seeking and some elements of your professional background, may be the same.

The samples given in Figures 14.4 through 14.6 demonstrate how to personalize cover letters for a variety of contact situations. Figure 14.4 is a standard cover letter used for answering advertisements from newspapers or professional magazines. Figure 14.5 shows a cover letter that reestablishes and builds on a previous professional contact. The letter in Figure 14.6 may be used for "blind" contacts (organizations with which you have had no prior contact). If you know someone in the organization, be sure to use his or her name in the letter as a means of introduction.

In seeking journalism positions, it is especially important that you show creativity and enthusiasm as part of your personality. But don't go overboard; too cute may seem unprofessional.

Cover letters should consist of the following elements:

1. A *salutation* to the person who can hire you. Most often, this is not someone in the personnel department.
2. The *opening,* something that catches the attention of the reader. Be creative! Introduce yourself and specify the job for which you want to be considered. If you have a referral name, by all means mention it, and if you are responding to an ad, state that. If possible, show your researching skills by pointing out something new or positive (or better yet, both) about the company.
3. The *body* provides a brief summary of your qualifications for the job and refers to the resume, which will reinforce your selling campaign to win an interview. Always stress what you can do for the company, not what you are hoping they will do for you.
4. In the *closing,* request an interview and state your intention to follow up with a call, preferably on a specific date. Use the standard "Sincerely yours" and type your name leaving room for you to sign in between. It's not a bad idea to put your address and phone number under your name in the event the letter gets separated from the resume, which has that information on it.

Clips

Most experts agree that when seeking a position in journalism, you should include clips (examples of your published work); some suggest two or three, others six to ten. Identify where each article or photo appeared. Try to show the quality and variety of your work. You may even wish to include a short paragraph of background information about each clip.

Portfolios

You may create a portfolio by organizing samples of your work: clips, projects, pictures, brochures, or whatever work best displays your talent for performing the job the employer needs. You may also include your resume, cover letter, addenda, and letters of reference.

Prospective photojournalists should include a variety of examples that are visually pleasing. Aspiring copywriters should include two or three campaigns featuring three ads for each campaign. All of these may be projects completed at the university level.

Audition Tapes

For those seeking a position in television, an audition tape is a necessity. It should be a montage of all your best work showing your reporting, writing, anchoring, producing, and editing skills. Your voice quality and intonation will be important, as will your creative efforts at putting the tape together in the best possible way. Tapes are usually necessary for those seeking jobs as reporters, anchors, sports reporters, and weatherpersons.

Figure 14.4 Sample Cover Letter in Response to an Advertisement

---

October 25, 19___

KKBT Radio
5600 Sunset Blvd.
Los Angeles, CA 90028
Attn: Liz Kiley, Operations Manager

Dear Ms. Kiley:

This letter is in response to your ad in *Radio and Records* for a program director. I've been paying close attention to your station's recent changes in programming and was excited to hear that you have gone urban.

I have had extensive experience in the world of radio over the past fifteen years. I have served in a variety of capacities, including program director/music director at WROB in Robinson, Illinois; producer/announcer at WGAU in Augusta, Georgia; and producer/announcer for WREE in East St. Louis, Illinois. I am a graduate of the Midwest School of Broadcasting. Though my background has been in smaller radio markets, I feel I am ready to break into a major market.

Enclosed is my resume. I look forward to seeing you for an interview and will be contacting you shortly.

Thank you for your time and consideration.

Sincerely,

Michael Ervin McDonald
333 E. Rhett Drive
Augusta, GA 33209
(404) 555-2108

Figure 14.5 Sample Cover Letter to a Personal Contact

October 30, 19 ___

David D. Geras
Director of Broadcast Operations
WGN-TV
700 W. Addison
Chicago, IL 60625

Dear Mr. Geras:

I enjoyed meeting and speaking with you at the Broadcast Careers seminar at Howard University last spring. I am writing to you now to express my interest in an opening at WGN for a News Assistant. I am enclosing my resume for your review.

Besides my recent B.A. degree in Journalism, I have gained experience over the last four summers in a variety of workplaces. Most recently, I completed an internship at WDC-TV in Washington, DC, where I assisted in the production of a news show. Previous internships include *Capitol Magazine, Chattanooga News*, and Park Advertising, Inc.

I would be glad to come to Chicago for an interview at your convenience. Thank you for your time and consideration.

Sincerely,

Terri Bakkemo
700 Thornborough Rd.
Chattanooga, TN 75221
(615) 555-2111

Figure 14.6 Sample Cover Letter to a Blind Contact

MARTHA WAYANS
4500 77th St.
New York, NY 10032
(212) 555-3839

May 5, 19 ___

George Jacobs
Human Resources
AT&T
1200 E. 5th Avenue
New York, NY 10019

Dear Mr. Jacobs:

Mitchell Sanderson, who works in the sales department at AT&T, suggested that I contact you regarding a possible opening in your public relations department. I am enclosing my resume for your consideration.

I will be graduating this month from New York University with a degree in Communications. My recent induction into the Communications Honor Society (Beta Alpha Psi) was a personal milestone. I am also a member of the Association of International Business (AIB).

I am interested in working in the communications industry in the field of public relations, and I feel that the best place for me to start would be at AT&T.

I will be calling you in about a week to follow up on this letter. Please feel free to call Mr. Sanderson for a reference. Thank you for your consideration.

Sincerely,

Martha Wayans

INTERVIEWING

The telephone rings: Your preliminary efforts have been rewarded. A prospective employer has called to schedule an interview. What a great time to sit around and wait for the day to arrive, right? *Wrong.* That's exactly what you should not be doing.

By the time you arrive for your interview, you should have used your research skills to find out all you can about the company, its recent history, and its plans for the future. It is also helpful to learn as much as possible about the particular position for which you will be considered. Then you will know, for instance, not to emphasize a desire to exercise your creativity when this job just isn't that kind of position.

Prior to the interview, you should go to the library and check business publications, regional and local newspapers, state manufacturing directories, *Barron's* and *Forbes* magazines, *Standard and Poor's Register,* the *Thomas' Register,* and trade or association publications that may have information about the company. You may also obtain information by calling the company's public relations or human resources department or the local Chamber of Commerce. When you arrive at an interview "armed" with information, you are apt to feel relaxed and in control.

You should also familiarize yourself with typical interview questions, including the following:

1. Why did you apply for this job?
2. Why should I hire you?
3. Why did you choose this career?
4. What would you do if…(fill in any related business crisis)?
5. What are your major strengths?
6. What do you see as your weaknesses?
7. What courses did you like best or least in school?
8. What would you like me to know about you?
9. Why did you leave your last job?
10. What are your goals?
11. What sets you apart from others who want this job?
12. What was your most significant job achievement?
13. Where would you like to be five years from now?
14. Where else are you interviewing?

Have a friend help you practice for the interview and use questions such as the ones listed above. Become comfortable with answering these types of questions.

Bring the following with you to the interview: several copies of your resume; a notebook or blank writing pad; pens; your own list of questions; clips or other samples of your work; your social security card, driver's license, and/or military records; and a reference list including names, addresses, and phone numbers, and any other names or information for former employers and schools. Organize everything inside some type of attache case or portfolio so that you have the appearance of a career-minded individual.

Arrive for the interview early. Dress in something comfortable but appropriate. For the most part, this means suits for both men and women. Employers are always seeking individuals who appear neat and clean. Remember, you need to establish a conservative, professional, confident image.

Establish eye contact with the interviewer and say: "Hello. I'm Mary Jones," not "Hi, I'm Mary." Don't refer to the interviewer by his or her first name even if asked to do so. Offer your hand for a firm handshake, whether you are male or female. Try to begin the interview on a relaxed note by mentioning something you know about the company or by pointing out something attractive in the office, perhaps a picture.

Be attentive. Answer questions as honestly and as fully as you can. Sound as if you are enthusiastic at the prospect of getting the job. No matter what questions you are asked, try to convey your ability to fulfill the responsibilities of the position and your eagerness and willingness to do so.

Here are some possible questions you might ask the interviewer:

1. To whom would I report?
2. What would a typical day on this job be like?
3. What training programs are offered?
4. (At a newspaper) How do you establish writing quality? How are training and feedback provided? What are the goals of the paper?
5. Does your company provide any financial assistance for furthering one's education?
6. Why did the last person leave this job?
7. What is the greatest challenge of this position?
8. How often are performance reviews given?
9. Are there a large number of team projects?
10. What kinds of assignments should I expect during my initial months here?

At the end of the interview, you need to know what the next step would be. If you are not told, you should ask. When would you be hearing from the company? Who might be the one getting in touch with you? Whom shall you get in touch with? When? When will a final decision be reached?

It's a good idea to write a thank-you note to the interviewer right after the meeting, thanking him or her once again. Reaffirm your interest in getting the job, your qualifications for being considered, and any new information that may add to the strength of your candidacy.

Once you are out of range of your interviewer, get out your notebook and jot down any notes you feel are important.

TESTS

On the day of the interview or at another time, you may be asked to take a test. Though this would be difficult to study for, it would be advisable to carefully read the *AP Stylebook*. You will probably be given sample text to edit to test your vocabulary, spelling, grammar, and punctuation skills.

For example, a newspaper chain in suburban Chicago includes a writing test for its prospective reporters that asks prospects to do the following: 1) Describe the most interesting person you've ever met; 2) Write a story based on the five facts you've been given here. 3) What questions would you ask someone who is celebrating his or her 100th birthday? Editors remark that the questions are open ended, drawing on the individual's own experience, and that, in conjunction with interviewing, the test provides insights into the capabilities of candidates. The Dow Jones Newspaper Fund has college professors write its "Controlled Editing/Writing Exercise," which all potential intern applicants are required to take. All tests evaluate verbal skills, journalistic style, and ability to create a news story under a deadline.

Some newspapers will require a tryout, meaning candidates are given a short period of time, perhaps three to six months, to display their abilities to handle the job.

FOLLOWING UP

If you haven't heard from a company within a week or two of the interview, feel free to call them. No, you won't lose your chances for a job by pestering them! Call the person who interviewed you or the last individual with whom you had contact. Tell him or her that you had not heard anything and wanted to find out if the job had been filled, when they might be making a decision, or if there was any additional information you could provide (references, more clips). It's true, the response may provide bad news; they may have filled the position with someone else. But even if that is the case, you now know you must move on and redouble your efforts to find other possibilities. Very often, though, a decision has not yet been made, and you created a positive atmosphere by showing your eagerness and enthusiasm for the job.

BUILDING A CAREER

You got the job. Congratuations! Now the work of building a career (or building your career further) begins. This is an ongoing process that never stops as long as you remain employed. You should always work toward expanding your horizons: take on additional responsibilities, learn new things, experience new happenings, strive for increased expertise, stretch yourself to new heights. You never know what you are capable of until you try to push yourself further.

As Chris Heide, Managing Editor of The Dartnell Corporation confides, "The best people in this business never stop learning; indeed, they are eager to learn more about everything they can every day. It's a never-ending process that takes constant practice and vigilance; while it may look easy to outsiders, those on the inside know the difficulties—and the rewards of the inner satisfaction it brings. The best people in this business listen more than they talk and know how to ask the right questions, of others and of themselves, to bring an inspired touch to what they write. You need a good ear for spoken conversation and a good eye for the written word. It takes dedication and discipline to please your harshest critic: yourself. The day you think you know it all is the day you start to decline. "Remember," says Heide with emphasis, "It's what you learn after you know it all that's really important."

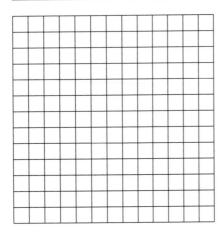

APPENDIX A: GLOSSARY

Advance Payment supplied before a manuscript is published and deducted from the author's royalty earnings.

Anthology A collection of selected writings by various authors or a number of works by one author.

Assignment A specific piece of writing that an editor asks a writer to produce for a particular fee.

Assignment Editor An editor who creates schedules and assigns reporters, and sometimes photographers, to stories.

B&W Abbreviation for black and white photographs.

Backlist A publisher's list of its books that were not published during the current season but are still available.

Best seller A book or other publication whose sales are among the highest in its group (such as fiction or nonfiction); the author of a best-selling book or other publication.

Bimonthly Every two months.

Bionote A sentence or brief paragraph about the writer. Also called a "bio," it may appear at the beginning or end of a piece of writing or on a contributor's page.

Biweekly Every two weeks.

Boilerplate A standardized contract. When an editor says "our standard contract," he or she means the boilerplate with no changes. Writers should be aware that most authors and agents make many changes to the boilerplate.

Bureau An agency or office for collecting or distributing news or information.

Byline The writer's name at the beginning or end of an article in a news-paper, magazine, or other publication.

Circulation The number of copies of a publication sold; the department responsible for distributing copies to newsstands, bookstores, sub-scribers, and so on.

Clean copy A manuscript free of errors, crossouts, wrinkles, or smudges.

Clips Samples, usually from newspapers or magazines, of a writer's pub-lished work.

Coffee table book An oversize heavily illustrated book.

Column inch The amount of space contained in one inch of a typeset column.

Commission To order a piece of writing, such as an article, to be done for a fixed amount of money.

Concept A statement that summarizes a screenplay or teleplay before the outline is written.

Continuity writing To write scripts, titles, and other introductory or transitional material for television shows or movies.

Contributor's copies Gratis copies of the issue(s) of a magazine or other publication in which the author's work appears.

Copy The manuscript that will be printed.

Copy editing Editing a manuscript for grammar, punctuation, and print-ing style, but usually not for subject content.

Copyright The exclusive, legally secured right to reproduce and sell writ-ten and other artistic works in the United States over a period of time.

Correspondent A person employed by a newspaper or broadcasting company to contribute regular reports from a distant location.

Cover letter A brief letter accompanying a manuscript or book proposal sent to an editor or agent; the letter accompanying a resume sent to a prospective employer. In all cases, it is a letter of introduction and ex-planation of who the writer is and where his or her talents and experi-ence lie.

Desktop publishing A publishing system designed for a personal computer.

Direct mail Printed matter sent directly to people's homes in an effort to obtain subscriptions or sales.

Disk A flat, round magnetic plate on which computer data is stored.

Electronic submission A submission made via modem or computer disk.

El-hi Elementary to high school.

Fair use A provision of the copyright law that says that short passages from protected material may be used without infringing on the owner's rights.

Feature An article that includes human interest rather than strictly news; a lead article or specific department.

Freelance writer A person who is paid only for each piece of writing published.

Fringe benefit A benefit, such as paid vacation time or medical insurance, provided by the employer in addition to salary.

Galley proof The first printing of a manuscript, usually in long sheets, used for correcting typesetting mistakes before the final printing.

Genre A general category of writing, such as novels or poems; subcategory of fiction (romances, science fiction, and mysteries).

Ghostwriter A writer who pens any work in someone else's name.

Hard copy The printed copy from a computer.

House organ A letter or magazine issued regularly to employees by an employer to provide information about the company.

Illustrations Photographs, engravings, or any other artwork.

Imprint Name applied to a publisher's specific line or lines of books.

Jargon Language and vocabulary peculiar to a particular group or profession.

Layout The arrangement of words, illustrations, and space in a newspaper, book, or other format to be printed or reproduced; also called "makeup."

Manuscript The handwritten or typed copy of an author's work prior to being typeset.

Masthead The standing heading in a newspaper (on the editorial page) or magazine (usually on the contents page) that contains the name of the publisher and other information about the publication.

On spec An article idea proposed to an editor by a writer. The editor may ask the writer to write the article "on speculation" meaning that, though the editor is interested, he or she is under no legal obligation to buy the manuscript when it is finished.

Payment on acceptance The writer is paid for work as soon as the editor accepts it for publication.

Payment on publication The writer is paid for work at the time of its publication (possibly months or even years later).

PR Abbreviation for public relations; the promotion of good will between a person, firm, or organization and members of the public.

Promote To increase public acceptance of a person or product through advertising and publicity.

Proofread To mark corrections on printer's galleys or other proofs.

Proposal In educational and other writing jobs, a report describing what work an organization will perform, including cost estimates, to solve a specific problem (for example, a proposal to conduct studies on language reading programs).

Public domain Material that was never copyrighted or whose copyright has expired.

Query A letter designed to promote interest in a writing project. Queries may be sent to editors and agents.

Rejection slip or letter A printed slip enclosed with a rejected manuscript returned by an editor to an author or the author's literary agent.

Remainder (verb) To sell the unsold copies of a publication at a reduced price.

Resume A French word meaning summary.

Royalties A percentage of the profit from the sales of a publication, paid to the author.

Scoop A news story first revealed by an individual, newspaper, or other source.

Script The manuscript of a play, motion picture, or radio or television broadcast.

Semimonthly Twice per month.

Semiweekly Twice per week.

Slant The approach or style of a story or article.

Stringer A reporter who serves a newspaper part time to report on special or local events and who only gets paid for the articles that are published.

Style The way in which something is written; for example, William Faulkner wrote in long descriptive prose whereas Ernest Hemingway used shorter sentences.

Subsidiary rights Authorization from a publisher to another company or companies to translate a publication or to produce it in paperback or as a movie, television show, and so forth.

Textbook A book used in the study of a subject, usually sold only through college bookstores or by the publisher's sales representatives to a school.

User friendly Easy to understand and make use of.

Vanity press or publisher A press that publishes books for which the author pays publishing costs.

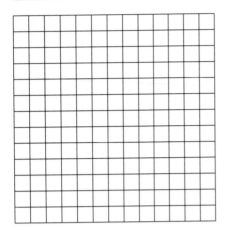

APPENDIX B: PROFESSIONAL ORGANIZATIONS

UNITED STATES

Advertising Club of New York
3 West 51st Street
New York, NY 10019

American Association of Advertising Agencies
666 Third Avenue
New York, NY 10017

American Association of University Professors
Suite 500
1012 Fourteenth Street, NW
Washington, DC 20005

American Book Producers Association
160 Fifth Avenue
Suite 604
New York, NY 10010-7000

American Society of Composers, Authors, and
Publishers (ASCAP)
1 Lincoln Plaza
New York, NY 10023

American Society of Journalists and Authors
1501 Broadway
Suite 302
New York, NY 10036

American Society of Magazine Editors
575 Lexington Avenue
New York, NY 10022

American Society of Newspaper Editors
Foundation
P.O. Box 17004
Washington, DC 20041

Associated Writing Programs
Old Dominion University
Norfolk, VA 23529

Authors Guild
330 West 42nd Street
New York, NY 10036

Dow Jones Newspaper Fund, Inc.
P.O. Box 300
Princton, NJ 08543

The Dramatists Guild
234 West 44th Street
New York, NY 10036

Editorial Freelancers Association
36 East 23rd Street
Room 9R
New York, NY 10159-2050

Education Writers Association
1001 Connecticut Avenue NW
Suite 310
Washington, DC 20036

International Association of Business
Communicators
1 Hallidie Plaza
Suite 600
San Francisco, CA 94102

International Television Association
6311 North O'Connor Road
Lock Box 51
Irving, TX 75039

International Women's Writing Guild
P.O. Box 810
Gracie Station
New York, NY 10028

Magazine Publishers of America
575 Lexington Avenue
New York, NY 10022

Mystery Writers of America
17 East 47th Street
6th Floor
New York, NY 10017

National Association of Science Writers
Box 294
Greenlawn, NY 11740

National Association of Broadcasters
1771 N Street, NW
Washington, DC 20036

National Association of Science Writers
P.O. Box 294
Greenlawn, NY 11740

National Conference of Editorial Writers
6223 Executive Blvd.
Rockville, MD 20852

National Newspaper Foundation
1627 K Street NW
Suite 400
Washington, DC 20006

National Writers Club
1450 South Havana
Suite 424
Aurora, CO 80012

National Writers Union
873 Broadway
Room 203
New York, NY 10003

New Dramatists
424 West 44th Street
New York, NY 10036

Newsletter Publishers Foundation
1401 Wilson Blvd.
Suite 207
Arlington, VA 22209

(The) Newspaper Guild
8611 Second Avenue
Silver Spring, MD 20910

Newspaper Association of America Foundation
The Newspaper Center
11600 Sunrise Valley Drive
Reston, VA 22091

PEN American Center
568 Broadway
New York, NY 10012
(branches worldwide)

Poetry Society of America
15 Gramercy Park South
New York, NY 10003

Poets & Writers
72 Spring Street
New York, NY 10012

Public Relations Society of America
33 Irving Place
New York, NY 10003

Radio–Television News Directors Association
1717 K Street, NW
Suite 615
Washington, DC 20006

Society of American Business Editors & Writers
c/o Janine Latus-Musick
University of Missouri
P.O. Box 838
Columbia, MO 65205

Society of Children's Book Writers
Box 66296
Mar Vista Station
Los Angeles, CA 90066

Society of Professional Journalists
P.O. Box 77
Greencastle, IN 46135

Society for Technical Communication
901 N. Stuart St.
Suite 304
Arlington, VA 22203

Songwriters Guild of America
276 Fifth Avenue
Suite 306
New York, NY 10001
and
6430 Sunset Boulevard
Hollywood, CA 90028

Volunteer Lawyers for the Arts
1 East 53rd Street
New York, NY 10022

Women in Communications
2101 Wilson Blvd.
Suite 417
Arlington, VA 22201

Writers Guild of America (East)
555 West 57th Street
New York, NY 10019

Writers Guild of America (West)
8955 Beverly Blvd.
West Hollywood, CA 90048

CANADA

Alliance of Canadian Cinema, Television
and Radio Artists
Writers Guild
2239 Yonge Street
3rd Floor
Toronto, ONT M4S 2B5

Canadian Authors Association
121 Avenue Road
Suite 104
Toronto, ONT M5R 2G3

Canadian Society of Children's Authors,
Illustrators, and Performers
Box 280
Station L
Toronto, ONT M6E 4Z2

League of Canadian Poets
24 Ryerson Avenue
Toronto, ONT M5T 2P3

Periodical Writers Association of Canada
24 Ryerson Avenue
Toronto, ONT M5T 2P3

Playwrights Union of Canada
54 Wolseley Street
2nd Floor
Toronto, ONT M5T 1A5

Writers Union of Canada
24 Ryerson Avenue
Toronto, ONT M5T 2P3

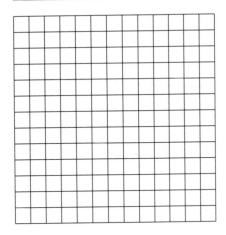

APPENDIX C:
RECOMMENDED READING
AND REFERENCES

Berkman, Robert I. *Find It Fast.* New York: Harper & Row, 1990.

Bly, Robert W. *The Copywriter's Handbook.* New York: Henry Holt and Company, 1985.

Burack, Sylvia K. (ed). *The Writer's Handbook.* Boston: The Writer, Inc., published annually.

Cantor, Bill. *Experts in Action—Inside Public Relations.* New York: Longman, Inc., 1989.

Carter, Robert A. *Opportunities in Book Publishing Careers.* Lincolnwood, IL: NTC Publishing Group, 1989.

Cutlip, Center, and Broom. *Effective Public Relations.* New Jersey: Prentice-Hall Inc., 1985.

Deen, Robert, *Opportunities in Business Communications.* Lincolnwood, IL: NTC Publishing Group, 1987.

Edelfelt, Roy A. *Careers in Education.* Lincolnwood, IL: NTC Publishing Group, 1993.

Edelstein, Scott. *The Writer's Book of Checklists.* Cincinnati: Writer's Digest Books, 1991.

Ellis, Elmo I. *Opportunities in Broadcasting Careers.* Lincolnwood, IL. NTC Publishing Group, 1986.

Ferguson, Donald L. and Patten, Jim. *Opportunities in Journalism Careers.* Lincolnwood, IL: NTC Publishing Group, 1990.

Fine, Janet. *Opportunities in Teaching Careers.* Lincolnwood, IL: NTC Publishing Group, 1989.

Foote-Smith, Elizabeth. *Opportunities in Writing.* Lincolnwood, IL: NTC Publishing Group, 1989.

Garvey, Mark (ed). *Writer's Market.* Cincinnati: Writer's Digest Books, published annually.

Gould, Jay R. and Losano, Wayne A. *Opportunities in Technical Communications.* Lincolnwood, IL: NTC Publishing Group, 1988.

Harrigan, Jane T. *Read All About It! A Day in the Life of a Metropolitan Newspaper.* Chester, CT: The Globe Pequot Press, 1988.

Hopper, Vincent F., Gale, Cedric, and Foote, Ronald C. *Barron's Essentials of English, 4th ed.* Griffith, Benjamin W. New York: Barron, 1990.

Leshay, Jeff. *How to Launch Your Career in TV News.* Lincolnwood, IL: NTC Publishing Group, 1993.

Lippman, Thomas W. (ed). *The Washington Post Deskbook on Style, 2nd ed.* New York: McGraw-Hill, 1989.

Noronha, Shonan F.R. *Careers in Communication.* Lincolnwood, IL: NTC Publishing Group, 1987.

Pattis, S. William. *Opportunities in Advertising Careers.* Lincolnwood, IL: NTC Publishing Group, 1986.

Pattis, S. William. *Opportunities in Magazine Publishing Careers.* Lincolnwood, IL: NTC Publishing Group, 1992.

Rotman, Morris B. *Opportunities in Public Relations Careers.* Lincolnwood, IL: NTC Publishing Group, 1988.

Tebbel, John. *Opportunities in Newspaper Publishing Careers.* Lincolnwood, IL: NTC Publishing Group, 1989.

VGM's Professional Resume Series. *Resumes for Communications Careers.* Lincolnwood, IL: NTC Publishing Group, 1991.

Yudkin, Marcia. *Freelance Writing.* New York: Harper & Row, 1988.

Zinsser, William. *On Writing Well, 4th ed.* New York: Harper and Row, 1988.

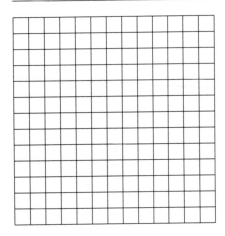

APPENDIX D: JOURNALISTIC ETHICS

In recent times, most professional organizations have adopted codes of ethics. The following represents part of *The Washington Post's* principles of standards and ethics for journalists. After Eugene Meyer bought *The Washington Post* in 1933 and began the family ownership that continues today, he published "These Principles:"*

The first mission of a newspaper is to tell the truth as nearly as the truth may be ascertained.

The newspaper shall tell all the truth so far as it can learn it, concerning the important affairs of America and the world.

As a disseminator of the news, the paper shall observe the decencies that are obligatory upon a private gentleman.

What it prints shall be fit reading for the young as well as for the old.

The newspaper's duty is to its readers and to the public at large, and not to the private interests of the owner.

In the pursuit of truth, the newspaper shall be prepared to make sacrifices of its material fortunes, if such course be necessary for the public good. The newspaper shall not be the ally of any special interest, but shall be fair and free and wholesome in its outlook on public affairs and public men.

---

*Above printed through the courtesy of *The Washington Post Desk-Book on Style, 2nd Edition,* compiled and edited by Thomas W. Lippman, McGraw-Hill Publishing Company, New York, 1989, page 7.

VGM CAREER BOOKS

CAREER DIRECTORIES
Careers Encyclopedia
Dictionary of Occupational
    Titles
Occupational Outlook
    Handbook

CAREERS FOR
Animal Lovers
Bookworms
Computer Buffs
Crafty People
Culture Lovers
Environmental Types
Film Buffs
Foreign Language
    Aficionados
Good Samaritans
Gourmets
History Buffs
Kids at Heart
Nature Lovers
Night Owls
Number Crunchers
Shutterbugs
Sports Nuts
Travel Buffs

CAREERS IN
Accounting; Advertising;
Business; Child Care;
Communications;
Computers; Education;
Engineering; Finance;
Government; Health Care;
High Tech; Journalism; Law;
Marketing; Medicine;
Science; Social &
Rehabilitation Services

CAREER PLANNING
Admissions Guide to
    Selective Business Schools
Beginning Entrepreneur
Career Planning &
    Development for College
    Students & Recent
    Graduates
Career Change

Careers Checklists
Cover Letters They Don't
    Forget
Executive Job Search
    Strategies
Guide to Basic Cover Letter
    Writing
Guide to Basic Resume
    Writing
Joyce Lain Kennedy's Career
    book
Out of Uniform
Slam Dunk Resumes
Successful Interviewing for
    College Seniors

CAREER PORTRAITS
Animals
Music
Sports
Teaching

GREAT JOBS FOR
English Majors
Foreign Language Majors
History Majors
Psychology Majors

HOW TO
Approach an Advertising
    Agency and Walk Away
    with the Job You Want
Bounce Back Quickly After
    Losing Your Job
Change Your Career
Choose the Right Career
Find Your New Career Upon
    Retirement
Get & Keep Your First Job
Get Hired Today
Get into the Right Law
    School
Have a Winning Job Interview
Hit the Ground Running in
    Your New Job
Improve Your Study Skills
Jump Start a Stalled Career
Land a Better Job

Launch Your Career in TV
    News
Make the Right Career Moves
Market Your College Degree
Move from College into a
    Secure Job
Negotiate the Raise You
    Deserve
Prepare a *Curriculum Vitae*
Prepare for College
Run Your Own Home
    Business
Succeed in College
Succeed in High School
Write a Winning Resume
Write Successful Cover
    Letters
Write Term Papers & Reports
Write Your College
    Application Essay

OPPORTUNITIES IN
This extensive series provides
detailed information on
nearly 150 individual career
fields.

RESUMES FOR
Advertising Careers
Banking and Financial
    Careers
Business Management
    Careers
College Students &
    Recent Graduates
Communications Careers
Education Careers
Engineering Careers
Environmental Careers
Health and Medical Careers
High School Graduates
High Tech Careers
Midcareer Job Changes
Sales and Marketing Careers
Scientific and Technical
    Careers
Social Service Careers
The First-Time Job Hunter

 VGM Career Horizons
a division of *NTC Publishing Group*
4255 West Touhy Avenue
Lincolnwood, Illinois 60646–1975